Kevin Clarke is a Chartered Surveyor who has worked in private practice in the UK, Middle East, Far East and USA. He lives in London and has attained MAs in Contemporary Theology in the Catholic Tradition and in Canon Law from Heythrop College in the University of London.

OFF-BEAM, OFF-SIDE, OFF-MENU

An Appeal From the Catholic Pews

Kevin Clarke

Book Guild Publishing
Sussex, England

First published in Great Britain in 2012 by
The Book Guild Ltd
Pavilion View
19 New Road
Brighton, BN1 1UF

Typesetting in Garamond by
Keyboard Services, Luton, Bedfordshire

Printed in Great Britain by
CPI Group (UK) Ltd, Croydon, CR0 4YY

A catalogue record for this book is available from
The British Library

ISBN 978 1 84624 685 2

Contents

Introduction

The rather unusual title to this book, *Off-Beam, Off-Side, Off-Menu*, has come to symbolise how I now perceive the Catholic Church.

By way of background, this is the Church into which I was born over 60 years ago and within which I was brought up by devout Irish parents. This is the Church whose teachings and practices shaped my early years, became something of a challenge as a teenager, but for the most part still exert a positive influence in my life. This is the Church in which I earnestly hope and pray that my children will persevere and in due course hand on their experience to yet another generation.

What, then, is the reason for my disquiet?

In simple terms, I believe we are *off-beam* in the way we continue to portray God and much of the import of the incarnation of Jesus. We are frequently prone to acting *off-side* in the manner in which we seek to control and manage this portrayal, and the unfortunate but inevitable result of all this is that the Church and its central message are becoming *off-menu* for an ever-growing number of people.

My use of the word 'we' serves as a reminder that through baptism each of us is called to promote the message of Jesus and to play our part in the building up of God's kingdom. In practice, the baptismal mandate for the majority of us only operates as a subcontract from the clergy, who are themselves under the auspices of a self-perpetuating pastoral leadership. This particular model of Church governance owes as much, if not more, to history as to theology and is far from being the most effective use of our collective talents.

During the course of my 60 years, Western society has witnessed significant change across a wide range of social and moral mores and this has been accompanied by major advances in the sciences and the application of technology. We have become an information-driven society with access to almost unlimited data at the touch of a button and we live in an interactive environment that allows and indeed promotes the idea of greater direct participation by the individual. This has produced a marked change in the way people tend to think and act, how they expect to be treated and how they respond to invitations to take an active involvement.

Over this same 60-year period, I have seen numerous friends and acquaintances drift away from active involvement in the Church or leave completely. For some this was a quiet departure and may not turn out to be a permanent breach, whereas others continue to carry the proverbial 'chip' on their shoulder. In society generally there is a noticeable attitude of indifference towards the Church as an institution with its teachings, or at least what is commonly understood to be its teachings, becoming viewed as less and less relevant to everyday life.

The official Church reaction is to lay the blame entirely on the growth of secularism in society and to attempt to close ranks against this and all other 'worldly philosophies'. Little obvious effort seems to be made to present authentic doctrine in the language of modern thought, and our pastoral leaders appear to be largely unaware of how poorly informed and sometimes confused many of the faithful are in respect of their basic beliefs.

I find this very sad and disappointing, and that is the reason why I decided to write this book. My aim is to highlight various teachings, practices, presumptions and omissions which give me cause for concern and which I suspect might well be contributory factors behind at least some of the recent defections from within the Church and our current negative rating in society at large. My template is the Second Vatican Council (Vatican II) which took place in the 1960s and brought together the bishops from around the world with the specific objective of examining the nature and purpose of the Church and its effectiveness in proclaiming the message of Jesus in the modern world.

Many of the Council's findings and their implications did not always generate unanimous support within the Church, and gave rise to several differing factions that tended to polarise under the broad banners of 'conservative' and 'progressive'. Generally speaking, the former were comfortable with the deemed certainties of belief and practice associated with the rigid and highly legalistic ecclesial structure that existed prior to Vatican II. The latter welcomed an opportunity to continue to explore and develop the Church's doctrine and liturgy within a less constricted environment.

It is a truism that the perfect religious organisation with the divine and the human in total harmony has never existed and never will.[1] An element of tension can often be a positive factor in our collective vocation, but it is the behaviour of the individual parties that will determine if or when this starts to become counter-productive. In the immediate aftermath of Vatican II, the verbal and literary confrontation between the differing factions was often condemnatory and sometimes extremely acrimonious. The majority of us at that time were unsure of many of the 'finer points' of contention and for the most part we were simply left to soldier on as best we could in the middle of this crossfire.

More than 40 years later, I believe that many of the scars which resulted from these earlier skirmishes have not fully healed. The players may have changed and the discourse become more muted, but sadly there are still too many occasions when expressions of opinion are accompanied by varying degrees of intolerance. In my view, this is a situation that needs to be better managed by our pastoral leadership for the sake of the present generation of the faithful who find themselves caught in this latest crossfire,

---

[1] Geoffrey Robinson, *Confronting Power and Sex in the Catholic Church* (The Columbia Press, 2007), p. 100.

and in order for us to present a more convincing picture to the world of the way in which we give witness to the message we purport to proclaim.

We need to appreciate also that there is no longer an automatic constituency for the Christian message and that we are required to compete with other 'concepts' in today's highly technical, highly funded and highly professional marketing environment. It is incumbent on us, and this means all of us within the Church, to develop a clear sense of purpose and equip ourselves to put into practical effect what it genuinely means to be followers of Jesus.

Our Christian witness has to involve more than mere conformity to a specified list of precepts, which is unlikely to impress Jesus any more now than it did in the Gospel accounts of his experience with the Pharisees. Nor is it simply promoting or supporting social or charitable causes, which are not of themselves unique to us or to any other religious affiliation. Our particular calling is to point to God through Jesus as the entire meaning of our lives and an offer of life for the whole of humanity. How much more could we achieve if we were to recapture the evident enthusiasm that this generated amongst Jesus' earliest followers?

This was the question that set the agenda for Vatican II and in my view continues to be relevant for us today when seeking answers to most of our present problems. We need to trace our steps back to Jesus as a person and make an effort to visualise how we might best translate his words and his actions into our contemporary words and actions, rather than just reading or listening to Gospel accounts. We need to become active evangelisers rather than passive consumer Christians. At the beginning of his public ministry, Jesus called for a change of heart and mind, but it was to people's hearts that his message was principally directed, for it was to become for them a whole new life experience of freedom and joy. This holds equally true for us today.

Against this background I have divided the book into three parts. Part One (Chapters 1–4) looks at God's gratuitous gifts to us, namely, creation, the incarnation of Jesus and the sending of the Holy Spirit. Part Two (Chapters 5–8) examines our response to God, which is essentially how the Church has developed and continues to implement the legacy which we received from Jesus. Part Three (Chapters 9–10) is a brief summary of what I consider to be our current effectiveness for purpose and some of the issues which I believe we might usefully examine in seeking to enhance our witness to Jesus in the future.

Part One

God's Gifts To Us

1

Once upon a Time

Question: Who made you?
Answer: God made me.

Question: Why did God make you?
Answer: God made me to know him, love him and serve him in this world and to be happy with him forever in the next.

These were the opening questions and answers in my *Penny Catechism*[1] when I began my formal religious education in the 1950s. The next few entries explained that I had been made in God's image and likeness, which could be found chiefly in my soul because, like God, it is a spirit and therefore immortal. In order to save my soul, I must believe in God, hope in God and love God with my whole heart.

Nothing here presented me with a problem. In a happy family environment with loving parents, it was very easy to visualise a loving 'Father' in heaven who had created all the good things around us and who counted us as his children. In return, we were simply to show him our gratitude by the way we lived and in particular by the manner in which we treated other people.

The starting point for me therefore was the faith story imparted

---

[1] *Catechism of Christian Doctrine* (Catholic Truth Society). Affectionately known as the *Penny Catechism* as a result of its one-time price. It is currently in print at £1.50.

by my parents and their day-to-day witness to this belief, which was a perfect foundation at the time and an ideal stepping stone for later life. But what of those who receive little knowledge of God from their parents, who are from broken homes or without a stable family environment? They may have no experience of love or a sense of belonging, which for them could remain purely abstract concepts and God – if ever thought of at all – viewed as a somewhat obscure and remote entity.

One of the consequences of this in society at large is that discussions on many of the major issues of the day tend to be confined to identifying practical solutions such as improving schools, hospitals and housing, reducing crime and the trafficking of drugs, minimising disparities of wealth, controlling immigration, adjusting environmental priorities, and so on. These are important topics in their own right, but in my view more fruitful and sustainable answers for human problems need to incorporate a spiritual dimension relating to each person; spiritual in the sense of that which links all the different facets of life into one whole in order to produce a sense of meaning to that whole.

The search for meaning is one of the most profound drives within human beings and there are few things that so eat away at a person's dignity and self-esteem as the loss of a sense of meaning in life. Society of late has been very effective in eliminating or minimising many of the spiritual values of the past, but seemingly less efficient in replacing them with other values which young people in particular find inspirational.[2]

Our contribution to the cause of the 'common good' must surely be to highlight this spiritual dimension which we believe is an intrinsic part of our human make-up – to emphasise that it is not an add-on or a bonus which attaches only to those who claim to be followers of a particular religious belief, but applies to every human person as a result of our being created in the

---

[2] Robinson, *Confronting Power and Sex in the Catholic Church*, p. 33.

image and likeness of God. This is an act of love which thereby confers a dignity on each individual.

We need to find ways to express this belief in contemporary terms and using contemporary language in order to attract the attention and interest of today's society. Success will not be achieved by issuing doctrinal statements in isolation, but rather by how people see us behave in response to these teachings, how they shape our lives and influence the way in which we treat others. I am not wholly convinced that the current approach and the choice of language adopted by our pastoral leadership is always conducive either to strengthening and expanding the faith of those who have one, or to successfully introducing the concept to those who do not.

God and creation

The *Modern Catholic Encyclopedia* defines 'God' as an object of worship and faith and an irreducible centre of meaning, power and value. It is also stated to be a proper name relating to the 'One' who creates, who thereby gives value to everything that has been created and who continually sustains all that is.[3] It is possible from this to say that the Christian God is a single identifiable God who is transcendent (rising above, surmounting all) in capacity and immanent (ever present, abiding) in application.

I remember as a schoolboy struggling with the notion that God had no beginning, that he always existed and will continue to exist for ever. God's future existence was perhaps the easier of the two to grapple with, as it only called for a projection beyond one's own time horizons, whereas attempting to understand how there was never a time when God did not exist was guaranteed to produce brain spasms.

---

[3] *Modern Catholic Encyclopedia*, eds. Michael Glazier and Monika Hellwig (Gill and Macmillan, 1994), p. 347.

By contrast, the Bible story of the emergence of Adam and Eve on day six of the first week of creation called for little mental exertion. It seemed wholly logical that God would wish to set in motion a sequence of events such as the provision of night and day, water and land, food and other animals in order to sustain and assist our eventual arrival. However, despite these facilities at their disposal, we were told that our first parents quickly managed to 'blot their copybook' by disobeying God's explicit instructions, and as a result they were forced to leave the comfortable surroundings of the Garden of Eden. It was intriguing at this early age to learn of parents being caught out and punished for doing something they had been told not to do!

Today I find myself no closer to being able to grasp fully the 'infinity status' of God, which is outside human experience and beyond the capacity of our intellect and language to formulate a definitive explanation. I remain nevertheless in the realm of faith, believing in a Creator God which for me is the most feasible and inspiring explanation of why and how we exist.

This is very much in line with the approach developed by St Thomas Aquinas (1225–74), traditionally known as the 'Five Ways', as a means to demonstrate the inner coherence of a belief in God. Belief is first assumed that the world mirrors God as its Creator, then the rational implications of this assumption are explored in terms of our experience of beauty, causality, signs of ordering and so forth, from which faith in God can be seen as offering a better 'empirical fit' with the world around us than any of its alternatives.[4]

St Thomas did not claim 'proofs' of God's existence, but rather that the appearance of design can offer persuasion concerning the divine creativity in the universe. This is obvious territory for an ongoing contest between religion and science, with the former basing its case on the Bible and an appeal to faith, and the latter

---

[4] Referred to by Alister McGrath and Joanna Collicut McGrath in *The Dawkins Delusion* (SPCK, 2007), p. 7.

claiming to offer convincing data which appeals to common sense. But are both 'sides' really arguing the same issue?

The answer in my view is not a simple 'yes' or 'no', as differing perspectives driven by different end objectives are frequently in play. To cite St Thomas Aquinas again, his contention was that truth is one because God, who is truth itself and the source of all that is true, is one. From this, it follows that any apparent contradictions between the content of revelation and the achievement of reason must be *only* apparent. Either the reasoning will turn out to have been a mistake, or the revelation will turn out to have been misunderstood.[5]

Thus the Bible describes creation as a sequence of events over a seven-day period with Adam and Eve arriving on the scene on day six once the necessary infrastructure was in place. In contrast, we are confidently informed by science that the start point for our universe was some 15 billion years ago, which triggered an ongoing and irreversible process that produced our planet earth (4 billion years ago) as one of several planets circling a major star we call the sun, which in turn is one of several million other similar stars in our galaxy. And how many more galaxies will be discovered beyond ours?[6]

This 'factual' account from science clearly rules out a literal interpretation of the Bible story, but does not negate its value as a 'figurative' account of the same event. In this regard, I recently came across a modern version from the theologian Michael Dowd, who adopted a 12-month calendar year as his time frame, in which:

The Milky Way galaxy self-organised in late February; our solar system emerged from the elemental stardust of an exploded super-nova in early September; planetary oceans formed in mid-September; Earth awakened into life in late September; sex was invented in late November; the dinosaurs lived for a few days in early December; and flowering plants burst on the scene with a dazzling array of colours in mid-

---

[5] *Modern Catholic Encyclopedia*, p. 792.
[6] Michael Morwood, *Tomorrow's Catholic* (Spectrum Publications, 1997), p. 22.

December and the universe began reflecting consciously in and through the human, with choice and free will, less than ten minutes before midnight on 31st December ... We have known we are in fact the Earth thinking about itself for only the last few seconds.

On this scale of 12 months, Jesus would be born on 31st December at 11:59:45 p.m. The major scientific discoveries of this century [20th and 21st centuries] would be in the final second before the end of the year.[7]

Similar to Genesis, this account adopts a descriptive currency to which people can easily relate and within which we are now able to include scientific factors which were not available to the original author. There is still no irrefutable proof of the existence of God, but, as indicated previously, I find the concept of a deity purposely willing a 'Big Bang' and all that has occurred subsequently to be more inspirational than the alternative and wholly abstract proposition that protons and neutrons just happened to interreact at a random point in time. Moreover, with the alternative proposition I am also prompted to enquire where these said protons and neutrons themselves are thought to have come from in the first instance.

Effectively, religion and science seek different answers about our world. As described by Ernest Lucas, science will ask how the world came about and may answer in terms of the 'Big Bang' theory, whereas Christians will be more interested in why the universe is here at all and answer this in terms of a Creator God and his purposes. Science is concerned with the physical world of material things and events and looks for explanations concerning matter and energy that can be counted, weighed and measured to see how it works – namely, its mechanism.[8] Religion seeks answers to such things as meanings, purposes and values.[9]

If these respective 'job descriptions' are acceptable, it seems to

---

[7] Referred to by Morwood, ibid., p. 28.
[8] Ernest Lucas, *Can We Believe Genesis Today?* (Inter-Varsity Press, 2001), p. 14.
[9] ibid., p. 31.

me that religion and science have a legitimate place alongside each other in the human quest for truth and meaning and should be capable of engaging in a mutually enriching dialogue while continuing to pursue their individual areas of expertise. Writing in the 1940s, Albert Einstein held that:

> Science can only ascertain what is, but not what should be and outside of its domain, value judgements of all kinds remain necessary. Religion on the other hand deals only with evaluations of human thought and actions; it cannot justifiably speak of facts and relationships between facts. According to this interpretation the well known conflicts between religion and science in the past must all be ascribed to a misapprehension of the situation which has been described.[10]

Part of the problem is that respective disciplines have been prone to adopt an 'energetic' stand-off approach. The dispute between the Church and Galileo is a well-known case in point. In this example, the scientific proposition that the earth travels around the sun rather than being the fixed centrepiece of creation was opposed on the grounds that it was in direct conflict with a literal translation taken from the Bible. It was several centuries before the Church formally apologised for its treatment of Galileo.

So how do we stand in this regard today? The Vatican II document 'The Pastoral Constitution on the Church in the Modern World' (*Gaudium et Spes*) confirmed that if methodical investigation in any branch of knowledge is carried out in a genuinely scientific manner and in accord with moral laws, it need never be in conflict with the faith, because the things of the world and the things of faith derive from the same God as do the 'humble and persevering investigators' (*GS* #36). The document goes on to criticise short-sighted attitudes concerning the rightful autonomy of science

---

[10] From the website *Albert Einstein, Religion and Science* (www.sacred-texts.com/aor/einstein/einsci.htm). A symposium published by the conference on Science, Philosophy and Religion in the Democratic Way of Life Inc., New York, 1941.

which from time to time have occasioned conflict and controversy and misled many into opposing faith and science.

Addressing the Pontifical Academy of Science in 1981, Pope John Paul II stated, 'The Bible itself speaks to us of the origins of the universe and its make-up not in order to provide us with a scientific treatise but in order to state the correct relationship of man with God and with the universe. Sacred Scripture wishes simply to declare that the world was created by God and in order to teach this truth it expresses itself in terms of the cosmology in use at the time of the writer.'

These are two examples which in my view represent a helpful and non-combative viewpoint from a religious perspective. More recently, the 1994 *Catechism of the Catholic Church* describes creation as being ordered (#299), having its own goodness and proper perfection, and being in a state of journeying towards an ultimate perfection yet to be attained to which God has destined it (#302). God is stated to be the sovereign master of his plan but willing to allow his creatures the opportunity to participate in its accomplishment (#306).

The process by which God guides his creation is defined as 'divine providence', which is explained as caring for all, from the least things to the great events of the world and its history, and being both concrete and immediate (#303). I am not entirely sure what this means and I can find no guidance in the text on how the concept is understood to operate. In other words, is divine providence an inbuilt element of God's design that predetermines how each event will and indeed *must* unfold, or can human freedom exert any real effect?

A similar question might be tabled by the scientist to determine what role, if any, a 'chance' or 'random' event plays in the fundamental process of the universe, from atomic physics through to genetics. In this context, a chance event is one which science cannot predict or which can only be predicted by mathematical probability, but may nevertheless raise questions concerning traditional scientific thinking and Christian teaching about a purposeful creation.

In today's world of science, the known existence of objectively random factors rules out the earlier mechanistic view of the universe as being in the nature of a gigantic clockwork which runs in a completely predictable manner until it runs down. Genuine novelty is now seen to be possible and sometimes actual; the future is not predetermined and human freedom can exercise a real effect.

The way in which this is explained is, of course, important. If chance is credited with being a positive force or itself a cause, it could be possible to argue that the universe is ultimately irrational with no rhyme or reason for why anything occurs – it just does. The fact that humankind happens to have evolved might also be considered purposeless or meaningless, along with everything humans do. Clearly such a viewpoint is wholly incompatible with Christianity and with our belief in a Creator God with a divine purpose. What may appear to us to be random within our current knowledge horizons could be entirely predictable and purposeful for God.[11]

Evolution

According to the Bible, God 'introduced' a new species on the sixth day of creation, namely, Adam and Eve, whom he placed as fully grown adults in a pre-prepared environment. This humankind, as described by the *Catechism*, is created in God's own image (#355), the only creature willed for its own sake and able to share by knowledge and love in God's own life (#356).

First man is stated to have been created good and established in friendship with his Creator and in harmony with himself and with creation around him (#374), and in an original state of holiness and justice in order to share in divine life (#375). First man was unimpaired and ordered in his own being because he was free of the triple concupiscence that subjects him to the

---

[11] *Modern Catholic Encyclopedia*, p. 302.

pleasure of the senses, covetousness for earthly goods and self-assertion contrary to the dictates of reason (#377).

We could conclude from this that humankind is a highly specified and privileged species and installed as such by God to take pole position in his plan for creation. In contrast, the 'theory of evolution' considers the possibility of a different route by which humankind secured its ascendancy and is concerned with explaining 'why' each species is as it is by proposing a general unified account of how different species are related.[12]

The term 'evolution' is usually associated with the naturalist Charles Darwin (1809–82), whose findings were that species do not always remain the same over time. They are mutable and undergo repeated changes and adaptations to their environment. Darwin's publication *On the Origin of Species* (1859) and the later *Descent of Man* (1871) generated another 'Galileo-type' reaction from many Christian Churches who viewed these works as being in direct contradiction to the Bible.

It is commonly acknowledged that evolution is not a proven, demonstrated certainty, but because there is so much that the theory does explain, biologists are virtually unanimous in accepting it.[13] The inevitable question, therefore, is whether this has to be in automatic conflict with the Christian doctrine of creation and specifically our human presence on earth?

The answer, in my opinion, will depend on the terms of reference which we adopt. If we insist on a literal reading of the Bible, we will have to conclude that the scientific community is wrong or that the available evidence can be explained in a different way. Alternatively, if, in the words of Pope John Paul II quoted above, we treat the primary reason for the story in Genesis as something other than a purely physiological account of origins, a meeting point is possible.

As this is described in the *Encyclopedia*, the doctrine of creation

---

[12] ibid., p. 301.
[13] ibid.

is not a story about the beginning of the world; it is a statement of belief that each thing that exists does exist and each event that occurs does occur because God knows and wills its existence and occurrence. In other words, creation is not itself an event in time, something that happened once but has now finished happening. It is a relation of dependence such that neither the universe as a whole nor any of its component parts, including biological evolution, is entirely self-explanatory. The only complete explanation of why things are as they happen to be is that God creates them so.[14]

On this basis, I believe we are able to assert convincingly that creation – which is generally agreed to have come into being from nothing – must, by necessity, be wholly permeated with God's presence as this is the only source from which it could have derived its existence in the first place. Within this broad understanding it then becomes possible to view the entire universe as one single process of evolutionary development, moving from 'Big Bang' through elemental particles to molecules to organisms to persons.

In the words of the American theologian Sally McFague:

All of us living and non-living are one phenomenon, a phenomenon stretching over billions of years and containing untold numbers of strange, diverse and marvellous forms of matter – including our own. The universe is a body, to use a poor analogy from our own experience, but it is not a human body; rather, it is matter bodied forth, seemingly infinitely, diversely, endlessly, yet internally as one.[15]

This echoes St Paul's account of God as Father of all, over all, through all and within all, who descended to the lowest regions of the earth so that rising he might fill all things (Ephesians 4:9–10). It was this Pauline passage that strongly influenced the

---

[14] ibid., p. 301.
[15] Referred to by Morwood in *Tomorrow's Catholic*, p. 39.

twentieth-century Jesuit theologian and scientist Teihard de Chardin (1881–1955) in his search to resolve the two apparently conflicting attractions of the impersonal world of matter known by science and the revealed word of God known by faith.[16]

Thus, through St Paul, we have revelation telling of God descending into the world of matter and we have science telling through the theory of evolution how matter rose into spirit – how the once impersonal world of matter became reflectively conscious as ourselves, rather than humankind being viewed as an entirely separate species from the rest of creation which was 'independently installed' at some point in time during the last 4 billion years.[17]

Within this model, the whole of creation can be seen to be infused with, sustained by and driven by the energy that is of God, and this has to make humankind more intimately related to God than being simply a physical end product. This relatedness is a key element in the theology of another twentieth-century theologian, Karl Rahner (1904–84), who regarded our relatedness to God as being so deeply built into us, so absolutely critical in making us what we are, that nothing we do would be possible without it. In Rahner's view, being related to God, whether we realise it or not, is so much part of our structure that it is not possible properly to describe what it is to love or what it is to will or even to think in a perfectly human way without bringing God into the description.[18]

This is not a statement of what God *is* and it may not necessarily coincide with the view of every scientist specialising in quantum physics, but from a Christian perspective it does suggest how we might better approach the notion of God being present everywhere. Here God is understood not as an external and remote overseer or manipulator of events who rewards and punishes, but as having an incarnational presence that operates in, with and through what God has to work with – namely, each of us.

How often are we reminded that we are 'created in God's

---

[16] *Modern Catholic Encylopedia*, p. 852.
[17] Michael Dowd, quoted by Morwood in *Tomorrow's Catholic*, p. 40.
[18] Karl Rahner, quoted by Karen Kilby in *Karl Rahner* (Fount, 1997), p. 2.

image', but without really thinking this through? If we treat the whole of creation as permeated with the presence of God, the wonder for us as humans is that we are conscious of this presence and can give it a name. As described by Michael Morwood, we can identify ourselves in terms of its reality, devise significance and give meaning to our lives, marvel at who and what we are, give praise on behalf of all creation and allow this faith to shape our lives and the destiny of life on this planet.[19]

As a result, we can and indeed should applaud rather than oppose advances in science which afford us an improving insight into the workings of God's plan for creation and the theology of human work, growth and achievement. This was well expressed by Frederick Templeton, Archbishop of Canterbury at the beginning of the twentieth century, who, when asked about the implications of the theory of evolution, is reported to have replied, 'We used to believe in a God who made things. Now we must believe in a God who made things make themselves. Which God is the more awesome given these circumstances?'[20]

We have a contribution to make in the process of human discovery and also a responsibility to ensure that the 'autonomy of earthly affairs' does not overlook what we regard as our underlying relatedness and dependence on God – to prevent the 'Big Bang' and everything that has followed being treated as an entirely material consequence, thereby excluding or at least casting doubt on the existence and importance of the inbuilt spiritual dimension which we attribute to the human soul.[21]

Original sin

The story of Adam's and Eve's disobedience came early in our religious education programme. It was preceded by a story about

---

[19] Morwood, *Tomorrow's Catholic*, p. 36.
[20] Referred to by Lucas, *Can We Believe Genesis Today?*, p. 26.
[21] *Modern Catholic Encyclopedia*, p. 302.

certain angels led by Satan who revolted against God's authority and, having been expelled from heaven, resolved to seek out easier targets of the human variety. In due course our first parents were tempted to disobey God and, as described in Genesis, they took and ate the fruit from the tree in the middle of the garden which they had been explicitly told not to do (Genesis 3:15).

As an explanation of evil, this first or original sin committed by humankind ultimately developed into the concept of 'original sin' – a central topic of Catholic teaching which was proclaimed a doctrine of faith by the Council of Trent (1545–63). It was presented there as a personal sin on the part of Adam resulting in the loss of a state of original justice and holiness, wounding the human nature passed on to his descendants, darkening their understanding, weakening their will and leaving them subject to pain and death. It is a condition of guilt found in all humans (excluding Mary, the mother of Jesus) prior to any act of sin on their part.[22]

Throughout Jewish history there had been a recognition of the inherent sinfulness of humanity and its need for salvation, but the Old Testament contains no explicit teaching about a primeval sin which was passed on to later generations. St Paul spoke of sin as a condition of human nature, something inside us and in conflict with our inner being, which can cause us to do things we hate rather than the things we want to do (Romans 7:15–20). In contemporary speech we might express this by saying that 'the spirit is willing but the flesh is weak'.

I believe it could be argued that the strong emphasis on sin by St Paul (see particularly Romans 3:12–20) may well have led to later theology reading Genesis as a literal description of the first sin and the fall of humanity. The term 'original sin' was actually coined by St Augustine in the early fifth century as a means of supporting his defence of orthodox Christian teaching against the heresy of Pelagianism, namely the claim that human

---

[22] ibid., p. 621.

beings can save themselves by virtue of their own free will and independently of divine grace – what became the concept of self-justification.

The theologians of the Middle Ages transposed original sin into an historical sequence of events in which our first parents were seen to have been created in grace, endowed with preternatural (i.e. beyond what is normally found in nature) gifts such as clarity of mind, strength of will and freedom from pain and death. Having failed the test of obedience, however, they lost their privileged state and then required the redemption of Christ.[23]

Whatever one's personal view of original sin, there is no way of avoiding the official teaching of the Church from the Council of Trent, but as with all official pronouncements, this teaching is the product of the culture and theology of the time. The Council of Trent had been convened to reassert 'traditional' Catholic teaching in the face of the Protestant Reformation in Western Europe, which amongst other areas of disagreement included a range of issues involving sin, grace and justification.

If one distinguishes between the substance of the Council's teaching and the formulations which were considered appropriate to meet the prevailing circumstances at the time, it would seem, in the words of the *Encyclopedia*, that the substance of faith could be summarised in statements that (i) Christ is at the very centre of the divine plan; (ii) all human beings have a basic need of the redemption he brought about; and (iii) this need is antecedent to any act of sin on their part, or even mere exposure to a sinful environment.[24] This seems to me to be a much closer 'fit' with the earlier view expressed by St Paul.

In contrast, the 1994 *Catechism* acknowledges that the description in Genesis is figurative, but affirms nevertheless that this was a primeval event, a deed that took place at the beginning of human history which is forever marked by the original fault, freely

---

[23] ibid.
[24] ibid.

committed by our first parent (#390). This fault is stated as being a deliberate act which cannot be explained away as a development flaw, a psychological weakness, a mistake, or the necessary consequence of an inadequate social structure (#387).

One wonders what prevailing circumstances could have been thought to apply at the end of the twentieth century in order to give rise to these latest formulations? In any event, the consequences of Adam's action are shown to be immediate and extensive. Adam and Eve lose the grace of original holiness; they become afraid of God, of whom they have conceived a distorted image – that of a God jealous of his prerogatives; their harmony is destroyed; the control of the soul's spiritual faculties over the body is shattered; the union of man and woman becomes subject to tensions; harmony with creation is broken; visible creation becomes alien and hostile; death makes its entry into human history (#399/400).

This 'litany of woes' is presented as the unavoidable inheritance we are called upon to accept as a result of our common lineage with Adam and Eve. Their personal sin is stated to have affected the human nature that they would transmit in a fallen state, which for us would be a sin that was 'contracted' and not 'committed'. It is a 'state', not an 'act' (#404).

I have to admit that the concept of guilt by association always seemed unfair to me as a child and contrary to my parental teaching on forgiveness without continuing to hold a grudge. The consequence of being without baptism as the means to exonerate this 'contracted state' was also presented in graphic terms, with 'limbo' on offer as the sole option for those who died without the sacrament. It is perhaps a sobering thought that on this proposition, well over half the population of the world – more than 3 billion souls – could be destined for nothing more than limbo.

In the light of what science has to say of human origins, I find this present *Catechism* teaching of a cataclysmic sin at the dawn of human history, with its immediate and ongoing implications, increasingly difficult to reconcile in this exact form.

Where, for example, is the evidence from Revelation of a specific primeval event that must be handed on? When was there a period of harmony in the history of the world that suddenly changed to become what we now know? Was there no death before our first parents?

In my view, we risk obscuring the underlying purpose of this teaching by the way it is currently presented, which, as suggested by the *Encyclopedia*, leaves a negative streak in the Church's psyche.[25] The message we should be emphasising is that in Christ there is the fullness of forgiveness and healing for the whole of creation, and I consider that this is ideally expressed by the main title of the relevant section in the *Catechism*, namely, 'When Sin Abounded, Grace Abounded All the More' (p. 86). It seems unfortunate that later in this same section comes the warning that we cannot 'tamper' with the revelation of original sin without undermining the mystery of Christ (#389).

In summary, I believe that the whole of creation is the product of a single defining purpose – a purpose which I refer to as 'God'. For me, this is a personal God who is distinct from the physical universe, but whose abiding presence permeates and sustains everything that has been brought into existence and provides the explanation for all that I am able to see and experience. As succinctly expressed by St Thomas Aquinas, we do not know *what* God is, only *that* God is. We know God only from God's effects.[26]

What we call the laws of nature are therefore expressions of God's activity in the world. They come with an invitation for us to participate and a freedom to choose whether we wish to accept or reject the offer. This ability to choose again serves to highlight the 'added dimension' which forms an essential part of our human make-up and which could not exist other than as a result of our specific relatedness to God.

Over recent centuries, science has progressively captured the

[25] ibid.
[26] Referred to by Catherine Mowry LaCugna, *The Trinitarian Mystery of God* (Fortress, 1991), p. 158.

middle ground of public opinion in claiming to provide definitive answers to questions concerning our world by methodical process rather than relying on mere hypotheses, which are often suggested as being all that is effectively on offer from the Church. From my position in the pews, we seem to have lost ground in relation to the scientific take on the story of creation by a tendency to treat new findings with suspicion or as a potential threat to Christian orthodoxy, and in frequently seeking to impose our own viewpoint in areas that are outside our direct remit and competence.

We run the risk of becoming categorised as advocates for the so-called 'God of the gaps', who operates only in those areas that science has not yet managed to clarify but confidently expects to do so in time and thereby extinguish the concept of God altogether.

In reality, science appears to be becoming much more aware that the line between fact and theory is a 'fuzzy' one, that theories are attempts to make sense of facts, but that what we see as facts and how we assess them is affected by the theories we already hold (or reject).[27]

The example concerning Galileo, mentioned earlier, is a classic one. Modern findings continue to uphold his conclusion, but they no longer support the reasons he claimed at the time. As a result of methodical scientific process, none of his original 'proofs' are now judged to be valid, much less decisive.[28]

A further observation from the *Encyclopedia* is that scientists in general are beginning to recognise that science is far less objective than ordinarily thought and that it is unable to offer a total interpretation of reality. At the same time, theology is no longer regarded as a purveyor of outmoded and unscientific notions about the world, but as a potentially serious partner in dialogue with science, particularly in the field of epistemology, the theory of knowledge, and the critical study of its validity, methods and scope.[29]

---

[27] Lucas, *Can We Believe Genesis Today?*, p. 32.
[28] *Modern Catholic Encyclopedia*, p. 793.
[29] ibid., p. 795.

It seems to me that science is one faculty of the human gift of reason, and theology is another. The former seeks to explain *how* things work, the latter attempts to offer explanations concerning *why.* Both disciplines can, and in my view should, operate in concert, representing different sides of the same coin – perhaps sometimes in tension, but not in automatic or perpetual opposition. Why, I wonder, do we always give the impression of seeking to preserve a particular viewpoint because it happened to be at the limit of our understanding at some designated past date that history has long since superseded?

I consider that there is a largely untutored and sometimes muddled understanding of God within the Church, which for many people has never been developed beyond their childhood catechesis. There is also often a tendency to read and interpret Scripture in a literal fashion. These two factors can combine to produce an ill-equipped laity who find it increasingly difficult to instigate and sustain a productive religious dialogue in contemporary society.

We need to seriously re-examine the way in which we present our case for a Creator God, who for many people still retains the image of some form of aloof personage existing alongside the things of the world and calling on us from afar to afford continuing reverence and obedience. Speaking of such a God as having boundless love for each of us can sound rather hollow and unconvincing and is unlikely to enthuse a society that seems to have difficulties already with concepts such as love and fulfilment.

We should attempt instead to promote a greater awareness of our relatedness to God and what this means for us as individuals, and more particularly as individuals in relationship to each other and the world around us. We should be promoting an understanding that we do not have to search for God, because he is already present within us as an intrinsic element of what it means to be human. We should be encouraging people to realise that we do not have to try to impress God, because he loves us unconditionally for who and what we are personally, and that we owe it to each other to show similar regard in the way we exercise our human faculty of freedom.

To refer again to my *Penny Catechism*, this fulfilled a useful purpose in the past, but we require a different facility today which provides clear and cohesive guidance from our pastoral leadership with all the benefits of the latest biblical, historical and scientific advances that are now at our disposal. We need material that treats us as adults, but uses an approach and a vocabulary which recognise the disparity which exists between popular faith and church scholarship. I do not consider that the latest (1994) *Catechism* meets this criteria.

We need to become better informed in order to re-engage with the world, rather than attempting to function as a separate and wholly autonomous organisation. We have an essential message to convey and we should not fear working alongside science and other fields of endeavour to help shape humanity's collective progress towards truth. We can be confident that whatever new discoveries or advances are made in the future, they will only serve to enhance our current appreciation of the love and immanence of God in each of our lives.

2

The Incarnation

Christianity is about the life, death and resurrection of Jesus. We proclaim our belief at Mass each Sunday in the words of the Credo:

> Only Son of God ... eternally begotten ... of one being with the Father ... for our salvation He came down from heaven ... became incarnate from the Virgin Mary ... suffered death and was buried ... rose again ... ascended to heaven ... is seated at the right hand of the Father ... will come again in glory to judge the living and the dead.

These are the faith statements which we recite week in and week out, but how much attention is given to, or how much are we encouraged to consider seriously, the origins and meaning of these individual expressions? 'Eternally begotten', 'came down from heaven', 'ascended to heaven' – when we speak this way about Jesus, what does it tell us about him and the reason for his incarnation?

The traditional explanation

Referring again to my memory of religious education as a schoolboy, God was described as being 'pure spirit', but we were told that, because of who he was, this did not preclude him from taking on an earthly form. This did not strike me at the time as a major issue. After all, if God was able, single-handedly, to create the universe and everything in it out of nothing, then making himself present in the form of a particular person at a particular point in time seemed to represent a comparatively straightforward exercise.

The person in question was, of course, Jesus, who was described in our *Penny Catechism* as 'God the Son who was made man for us' (#32). Quite how this came about and how he 'juggled' the tasks of remaining truly God (#33) and being truly man (#37) fell within the 'too difficult to handle' category for 1950s schoolboys and was not an issue which we were encouraged to pursue in great detail. We were recommended instead to accept that for God everything is possible and to concentrate more on our share of the blame for Jesus' death and the rules of behaviour that we were now being called upon to follow.

The purpose of the incarnation, for Jesus to take on himself the nature of man, was stated as being 'to redeem us from sin and hell and to teach us the way to heaven' (#43). This required Jesus to suffer death on the cross in order to 'atone for our sins and purchase for us eternal life' (#55). A connection was made between the sin of Adam and the subsequent crucifixion of Jesus, with the explanation being that this was the necessary price to restore us to God's favour and to repair the breach in what had previously been the totally harmonious relationship between God and humanity.

So what is the picture which begins to emerge here? We start with God's gift of creation, which is recorded in Genesis as being 'good', but which our first parents quickly managed to blight by their act of disobedience. This offended God to the extent that his forgiveness called for suitable prior amends to be made. As we had become a 'flawed species' through the actions of Adam and Eve, we were unable to achieve this by our own efforts and so, in due course, God gave us a second gift in the form of his Son.

Jesus was dispatched to earth to become one of us, and to

suffer and die in order to wipe the slate clean of all previous sins and as payment on account for all future sins. God raised Jesus from the dead so that, as 'fellow human beings', we could again become eligible for the original offer of eternal life. The extent of God's love was evidenced by the suffering that his Son Jesus was called upon to endure on our behalf and we were left in no doubt as to the challenges we would be required to face and overcome as part of life's ongoing battle between the forces of good and evil.

Looking back to this period, it almost seems as if sin was the principal driver of events: the initial sin which led to our 'fall' from favour in the first instance, sins that each successive generation had committed and sins that we would inevitably succumb to in the future as a result of our now weakened human nature. Sin was categorised as 'mortal' (serious) and 'venial' (more easily pardoned). The souls of those who died in venial sin could expect to spend time in purgatory until they had fully paid the debt of temporal punishment due to those sins (#107), whereas the souls of those who died in mortal sin would go to hell for all eternity (#125) – strong stuff for impressionable seven- or eight-year-olds.

I well remember also the words of the 'Act of Contrition' which we were required to memorise before our First Confession: that sin deserved punishment, sin caused Jesus to be crucified and sin offended God. We could consider ourselves fortunate in being given a second chance through Jesus, but this came conditional upon our following an itemised litany of liturgical practices and at the same time avoiding a whole raft of moral prohibitions.

Failure to maintain a 'clean record' would serve as a constant reminder of our personal responsibility for Jesus' suffering and death and our continuing need to rely on God's mercy in order to minimise the punishment which might otherwise be due. Sound theology, perhaps, but considering the manner in which this was presented at the time, it is little wonder that most Catholics were perceived to be perpetually guilt-ridden and the Church as a whole judged to be travelling in an altogether different earthly orbit.

Over fifty years later, I consider that several aspects of this earlier teaching warrant a re-examination. First, the way the incarnation was presented could create the impression that the event was an afterthought and Jesus a time-specific contingency which had become necessary as a result of unexpected and continuing bad behaviour by humankind. In reality, there can be no question of God's plan for creation having to admit to surprises or the need for any mid-course corrections. He will have been fully aware from the outset of how human affairs would evolve.

Second, I seriously question whether we can or should talk of God being 'offended' in the manner usually associated with the use of the word, namely, concerning an affront to a person's pride or dignity. How is this possible when we are speaking about God? And yet the authorised prayer for use at confession called for us to detest sins most of all because they offended God's infinite goodness. It is difficult also to imagine that an offended God purposely willed such an extensive period of divine displeasure to elapse before being prepared to move towards a reconciliation in the form of the incarnation, but our *Penny Catechism* stated that even the just were precluded from heaven until this was opened for them by Jesus (#65).

Third, and for me the most uncomfortable aspect of our school teaching on the incarnation (or at least my recollection of it), was that Jesus' death was presented as its own self-description. In other words, it was a sacrificial act that met the predetermined criteria deemed to be necessary to make amends for our sins. By implication, therefore, it was an act that had been specified by God as his minimum reserve price for our redemption, for how else would the criteria have been identified, and for whose benefit otherwise was the price to be paid? What an astonishing view of God this represents.

From the earliest times in human history there is evidence of sacrifices being offered to appease a deity or to gain a favour. The Old Testament contains numerous references to gift-offerings, sin-offerings and communion-offerings and perhaps the most notable example was the recorded willingness of Abraham to consider sacrificing the life of his son Isaac out of obligation to what he understood to be the will of God. We know, of course, that God never intended Abraham to make such a sacrifice and was merely testing to see how obedient he was.

In the case of Jesus, and out of obedience to his understanding of God's purpose, he was prepared to sacrifice his own life. In one respect, he was not unique in facing an untimely and painful death as a result of pursuing a firmly held belief or inner conviction. Throughout history, the life expectancy for prophets has never been particularly encouraging and Jesus was in all probability aware of the risks when he first took up his public ministry. He resolved nevertheless to pursue his chosen agenda to its conclusion, whatever the cost.

In my view, however, there is a vast difference between a death which is presumed to represent a necessary end in itself and a death which follows as a result of what Jesus said and did. In the words of Gerald O'Collins, the self-sacrifice of Jesus was not due to his positive and direct will (or to that of his Father), but to the abuse of human freedom on the part of the religious and political leaders at the time whose vested interests were threatened by his uncompromising message.[1]

This distinction did not form part of our school agenda and for most of us the purpose of the incarnation was understood principally, if not exclusively, in the context of the passion and death of Jesus as a stipulated measure to placate God and thereby restore us to favour.

The present explanation

If the aforementioned was the experience of my generation, has the emphasis altered over the ensuing years? The 1994 *Catechism*

---

[1] Gerald O'Collins, *Jesus our Redeemer* (Oxford University Press, 2007), p. 171.

states that Jesus' violent death was not the result of chance in an unfortunate coincidence of circumstances, but is part of the mystery of God's plan (#599). So little apparent change here.

It then proceeds to describe the death of Jesus as the 'Paschal Sacrifice' that accomplishes the definitive redemption of man, and as the 'Sacrifice of the New Covenant' which restores man to communion with God by reconciling him to God through the blood of the covenant which was poured out for many for the forgiveness of sins (#613). The sacrifice of Jesus is explained as 'a gift from God himself who hands his Son to sinners in order to reconcile us with himself and his Son offers his life in freedom and love to the Father in reparation for our disobedience' (#614).

So what sort of picture of God does this create for the present generation of Catholics? In my view, much the same as for us before. The purpose of the incarnation continues to be identified chiefly with the crucifixion as a prerequisite to satisfy an apparently demanding God whose renewed friendship with humanity depended on adequate recompense in the form of pain and death. The entire initiative is seen to have been orchestrated by God, and this description of his Son's suffering and death appears to me to display an almost 'cultic' image.

My generation will not have considered it appropriate to question the officially presented explanation of the incarnation, but this is no longer the case with younger Catholics. They are likely seriously to wonder whether this is a worthy description for a God of infinite love and compassion. The answer must be a resounding 'no'.

Perhaps part of the problem is in the choice of language, stretching back to the time of the Gospels and incorporating the accretions and formulations which have occurred over the centuries. As indicated in the *Encyclopedia*, the early disciples of Jesus found the resurrection too big for any one theology and so they adopted a variety of images and metaphors in order to try to explain what God had done in Jesus.[2] These would have drawn heavily on

---

[2] *Modern Catholic Encyclopedia*, p. 784.

their Jewish scriptural heritage, together with the Hellenistic culture of the time, and their use of words such as 'salvation', 'redemption', 'justification', 'expiation' and 'reconciliation' will almost inevitably differ from our contemporary understanding.

As examples, the image at the base of the word 'salvation' (Greek: *soteria*) is that of a rescue from any form of harm. The great act of salvation in the Old Testament was the rescue of the Jewish community from slavery and exploitation in Egypt, which thereby established an understanding of the God of Israel as Saviour and Redeemer. Carried forward to the New Testament, the whole of Jesus' ministry can be seen as a constant witness to God as Saviour.[3]

The primary meaning of 'redemption' (Greek: *apolytrosis*) is a buying back, a ransoming of someone who had become a prisoner or fallen into slavery. In the thought world of early Christian communities, Jesus' death and resurrection might therefore be seen as God buying us back from sin and evil and taking us into a new relationship (1 Corinthians 1:30). This is fine as far as it goes, but over the years Jesus' death could easily become seen as a price which was paid to someone (e.g. God) or something (e.g. the Law). There is nothing in the New Testament to support such a view, which certainly extends the original metaphor well beyond St Paul's intended meaning.[4]

Centuries later, and to counteract theological mistakes of this nature, St Anselm (1033–1109) developed a theology of Jesus' death as an act of 'satisfaction', returning to God the honour stolen by human sin. 'Satisfaction' is a non-biblical term with roots in the feudal society of the time and relates to the principle of good order in society. As described by Richard McBrien, 'The feudal lord cannot simply overlook an offence which had been committed because the order of his whole economic and social world is at stake. So too, with God.'[5]

---

[3] ibid., p. 785.
[4] O'Collins, Jesus our Redeemer, p. 120.
[5] Referred to by Robert A. Burns, *Roman Catholicism after Vatican II* (Georgetown University Press, 2001), p. 18.

Despite St Anselm's explicit rejection of the notion of God exacting retribution by punishing his Son, the sacrifice of Jesus in terms of satisfaction did become seen over time as a particular form of justice, namely a penance which had to involve a punitive element. This opened the way to the idea of propitiating an angry God by paying a redemptive ransom, and in its severest form Jesus became seen as a penal substitute, burdened with the sins of humanity, judged, condemned and deservedly punished in our place, in order to satisfy divine justice.[6]

Sadly, I consider that traces of this mindset are often visible in the way that Catholic teaching on the incarnation is presented and understood. This seems to be based on an underlying presumption that the nature and exercise of divine justice has to mirror the way in which we have devised and apply our own human system of justice and retribution.

In order to reinforce the importance of language when attempting to describe the incarnation, Gerald O'Collins devoted the entire first chapter of his recent book *Jesus our Redeemer* to tracing the origins and development of the principal redemptive terms and images. He also cautioned against assuming that words with similar meanings are automatically interchangeable, on the grounds that individual words enjoy their specific denotations and meanings when used with other words in phrases, entire sentences or whole paragraphs.[7]

As examples, O'Collins shows that the emphasis in the use of the word 'atonement' has changed from its first understanding as a state or condition of being at one with others in a harmonious unity – 'at-one-ment' – to become a description which highlights the means for restoring harmony and the cost entailed in reconciliation.[8] The modern dictionary defines 'expiation' as making amends for a sin or wrongdoing, whereas scripturally there was never an understanding of sinners being able to do something in

[6] O'Collins, *Jesus our Redeemer*, p. 137.
[7] ibid., p. 3.
[8] ibid., p. 10.

order to placate or appease God. For us, it is God who lovingly deals with our sins through Jesus, which, as O'Collins rightly observes, says much about the image of God we should nourish and cherish.[9]

Finding a more balanced explanation

I believe that greater emphasis needs to be directed towards treating Jesus' life, death and resurrection as wholly interrelated components of a single God-given experience for humankind. The underlying purpose for the incarnation, for Jesus to become man, can therefore be seen as being to proclaim the reign of God and to show how a human person can and should live in accordance with God's original intention.

In my view, this is well expressed by the *Encyclopedia*:

> When Jesus ate with outcasts and sinners, when he ministered amongst the peasants of Galilea, when he challenged the religious and social patterns of exclusivity, domination and self-righteousness and replaced them with ones based on compassion and when he involved men and women in a radically inclusive community of disciples, God's salvation was already present and being made manifest.[10]

It is evident too from Jesus' healings that salvation was not restricted solely to the 'religious' areas of life, but involved liberation from all that oppresses and enslaves people. In the words of Michael Morwood, 'Jesus understood his ministry in terms of setting people free ... his life and death were not concerned with changing God's mind or winning back God's friendship. Rather, his living and dying were about changing people's minds and

---

[9] ibid., p. 17.
[10] *Modern Catholic Encyclopedia*, p. 784.

hearts... In Jesus' preaching, salvation is connected with setting people free from fear, ignorance and darkness and with changing the way they imaged and thought about God and themselves.'[11]

A further lesson from the story of the incarnation is that following Jesus is not an automatic recipe for an easy life. How often do we consider personal setbacks as unfair because we always claim to abide by the rules, or how often do we resent the good fortune of others who seem to have no regard for any moral or spiritual code? Consider Mary's positive response to the announcement by the Angel Gabriel that she had been specially chosen by God. This did not prevent her from having to spend the closing stages of pregnancy in transit, from giving birth in a stable, from being forced shortly thereafter to flee and remain in exile and later to be called upon to witness the cruel death of her son. 'Who', she might well have asked, 'needs friends like this in high places?'

As a result of the mystery of sin and evil in our world, Jesus was forced to suffer despite a life which was led in fidelity to God and in love for others, which he maintained without rancour up to the point of his death on the cross. In his resurrection, however, it is clear that the final say is emphatically with him. There is nothing now that need ever hold us captive other than the love of Jesus, who through his incarnation is well able to understand our daily concerns and appreciate the human pressures to which we are subjected.

People believed that they saw the divine operating in Jesus and the whole of his life made visible the 'art of the possible' for the rest of us. This was evidenced in the way it transformed the lives of some of his early followers such as St Irenaeus (d. AD 200), who spoke of 'recapitulation' – an historic process that moves towards a climax in which Jesus becomes the head of a new humanity standing in solidarity with his brothers and sisters. St Athanasius (d. AD 375) was a prominent representative of the

---

[11] Morwood, *Tomorrow's Catholic*, p. 79.

theology of 'deification', which held that the reason why Jesus who was divine became truly human was so that we as humans might be made divine by grace and adoption.[12]

The theology of deification continues to be a prominent element of teaching within the Orthodox Churches, but does also find its way into the *Catechism* of the Roman Catholic Church as one of a number of reasons which are given to explain the incarnation. Predictably, our list begins by describing Jesus' task to reconcile us with God by being sent to be the expiation for our sins (#457), to show God's love (#458) and to be our model of holiness (#459). But for me the final and most compelling reason which is listed warrants being quoted in full:

> The Word became flesh to make us partakers of the divine nature. For this is why the Word became man and the Son of God became the Son of man: so that man, by entering into communion with the Word and thus receiving divine sonship, might become a son of God. For the Son of God became man so that we might become God. The only-begotten Son of God, wanting to make us sharers in His divinity assumed our nature, so that he, made man, might make men Gods. (#460)

This is a truly breathtaking concept to try to come to terms with, and all the more so for those of us who were brought up on an extensive diet of human sin and failure. We were taught about being created in God's image, but this was generally understood to be confined to our souls which we continuously disfigured or damaged by sin, and so the whole good and bad scenario rolled on. The idea of an 'holistic me' forming a part of God's divinisation plan for humankind must transform the way each of us views God, our relationship with Jesus and our interrelationship with each other.

---

[12] *Modern Catholic Encyclopedia*, p. 820.

What a pity if the richness of this theology is lost because of the way these doctrinal formulations are currently presented. At best, the reason for the incarnation may be read as four equally rated explanations, although for my 'sin-obsessed' generation, I suspect that their individual importance will be assumed by the order in which they are presented. What a difference it could make if the final explanation – the divinisation of each of us – was to be offered as *the* defining purpose for the incarnation, thereby establishing an overall framework within which to rank and interpret the other given explanations.

In other words, rather than the starting point always seeming to be the sinfulness of humankind which requires God's continual pardon, our focus could be directed more towards God's unbounded love for each of us in whom he sees the image of his Son, Jesus. An example from the New Testament is the well-known parable of the prodigal son (Luke 15:11–32). Here we learn of a younger brother who leaves home and squanders his inheritance by engaging in activities wholly alien to his upbringing, but when he reconsiders this chosen way of life and decides to return home, there is no question of having to seek pardon, let alone offer recompense. All that matters for the father in this parable is his son's return. Forgiveness is automatic without the need to dwell on the reasons for the son's original decision. Why could we not refer to this instead as the parable of the forgiving father, given that the main purpose of the story is the forgiveness by the father, not the wastefulness of the son?

In my view, starting out on a positive footing is far more likely to improve our understanding of God's plan of salvation. We could then treat the divine activity of creation and redemption as distinguishable but interconnected moments, understanding that creation was planned with the coming of Jesus in mind, irrespective of what Adam might or might not have done (Ephesians 1:9–10). Centuries ago, St Irenaeus wrote of God creating Adam and Eve in order to have those on whom 'to shower the divine gifts'. As observed in our own time by Gerald O'Collins, if this was true of creation, it remains all the more true of redemption, which aims finally at the divinisation of humanity – drawing us into the inner life of God to share an existence of eternal love.[13]

I am not attempting to deny the presence of sin in the world, or to minimise its negative and debilitating impact. It is more a question of balance, of how and where the emphasis is placed. I believe this is an issue that needs to be addressed by our pastoral leadership.

We have a confessional attitude towards sin which still seems to be understood principally as a litany of declarable actions that have been individually defined and graded according to their deemed seriousness against God. For some people this can become an all-consuming and acutely worrying exercise of daily soul-searching for possible transgressions, whereas others may continuously look to find loopholes within the definitions to seek to avoid direct culpability.

This overtly legalistic outlook of defining and grading sin may well be one of the causes for the decline in personal confessions over recent years, particularly amongst the young, whose outlook on life can tend to be less 'black and white' than with earlier generations. The tragedy here could be that without the direct experience of God's presence in the sacrament of reconciliation there is the risk that the incarnation could simply be thought of as an event from history involving a rather abstract concept, rather than as the continuing expression of God's love and compassion. Contrast the almost universal feeling of peace, freedom and inner calm which can follow the making of each 'good' confession.

In summary, I consider that there are several confusing messages which follow as a result of the way the incarnation continues to be presented.

1.   We are taught that God is infinite love and compassion, but at the same time he is portrayed as requiring due

---

[13] O'Collins, *Jesus our Redeemer*, p. 183.

recompense for our sinfulness. Could this imply that God loved humanity less before the incarnation?

2. The death and resurrection of Jesus can be seen as high points in God's unfolding plan, but the emphasis which is often placed on the sacrificial nature of our deliverance from evil can result in salvation appearing to be a process or even a formula, rather than a person (or more correctly three divine persons) acting with boundless love. As this is expressed by Gerald O'Collins, 'The tri-personal God exercises causality on human beings and their world and does so in an utterly personal and loving way.'[14]

3. The focus of the incarnation can tend to be concentrated on Jesus' passion and death in isolation, thereby adding further weight to the notion of its sole purpose being to satisfy a remote and angry God. What could be further from the true picture of our God, whose forgiveness was never in doubt and who chose to express this in a manner which is compatible with our intrinsic human gift of freedom? In other words, Jesus freely undertook the role of devoting his entire life as an act of love for the sake of others.

4. While Jesus is described as both divine and human, the latter can come across as the 'junior partner' in this arrangement, minimising the inspirational impact of what he said and did throughout his life as he acted with a human will and loved with a human heart.[15] The stress on Jesus' divinity is understandable given that opposition to this belief has been the more prevalent over the centuries, but I consider that we need to recover a better balance in order to avoid Jesus only appearing to be human, a mythical divine simply acting out a human charade.[16]

---

[14] ibid.

[15] 'Pastoral Constitution on the Church in the Modern World' (*Gaudium et Spes*), #22.

[16] Burns, *Roman Catholicism after Vatican II*, p. 21.

5. The status of sin when expressed mainly as a codified
   format can easily exert an unhealthy influence that makes
   life appear to be a perpetual route march across a minefield
   of mortal and venial sins that are about to explode.[17]
   As mentioned previously, I am not doubting the existence
   of sin and evil and fully subscribe to the view of the
   Anglican Bishop of Durham, N. T. Wright, that if you
   pretend evil is not there you merely give it more space
   to operate.[18] However, it can be equally damaging to be
   totally preoccupied with the topic and, as succinctly
   suggested by Wright, 'evil' may well be a four-letter
   word, but so too, thank God, is 'love'.[19]

In this regard, how refreshing it is to read the view of the
Redemptorist theologian Bernard Haring that we are most like
God in our freedom. In Haring's words:

> We are created to be free to grow and develop into the
> fullness of the maturity of Christ. We do this by saying Yes
> to the world, to life, to our neighbour and in and through
> all of this to God. To say No, is to sin, is to alienate ourselves
> from the world, from life, from our true selves, from our
> brothers and sisters in the human family and ultimately
> from God who created us for life, for friendship and love.
> If the glory of God is the human person fully alive, sin
> can be seen as anything that violates our human dignity,
> anything that restricts or blocks freedom in ourselves and
> others.[20]

The paradox for me is that because of the way much of our
Catholic teaching on the incarnation continues to be presented,

---

[17] Robinson, *Confronting Power and Sex in the Catholic Church*, p. 27.
[18] N.T. Wright, *Evil and the Justice of God* (SPCK, 2006), p. 56.
[19] ibid., p. 56.
[20] *Modern Catholic Encyclopedia*, p. 805.

the institutional Church seems increasingly to manifest the sort of restrictive and self-righteous mindset that Jesus sought to dispel by virtue of his incarnation.

3

In Search of Jesus

The person of Jesus is central to the accomplishment of God's plan for creation. As described in the *Encyclopedia*, Jesus is who he is because of what he did, and what he did, he did in virtue of who he is.[1]

So who is this man and what do we really know and understand about him? Ask a group of Catholics to describe Jesus, and their ready answers will undoubtedly include 'God made man', 'the Son of God', 'the Word made flesh', 'the Second Person of the Blessed Trinity', 'Our Lord and Saviour'. Ask for a fuller explanation of one or more of these titles, and I suspect that a less immediate and less confident response could be forthcoming.

The reason for this, in my experience, is that official Church teaching has tended to comprise a litany of faith statements that have not always been accompanied by explanations of the context in which they might best be understood. For the most part this was not a problem for my generation as we tended simply to memorise and follow by rote, but this can no longer be assumed as a given. In today's climate, the 'why' and the 'how' need to form part of the basic proposition, as loose ends or perceived inconsistencies can easily become faith deterrents.

We call ourselves followers of Jesus and proclaim that he is head of the Church, but is there a consistent understanding of what we mean by this? Can the person of Jesus be seen to influence

---

[1] *Modern Catholic Encyclopedia*, p. 819.

our lives? How convincing are we in the example we give to others? Today's society is frequently referred to as being overtly secular and opposed to Christian values, which may well be the case for some people, but I suspect that the overwhelming majority of the population are simply content to go along with what is on offer in the absence of what they may see as a credible or inspirational alternative being offered by us.

I am not sure whether our pastoral leadership is aware of the degree of uncertainty which exists amongst the faithful concerning the person of Jesus and how this can inhibit our overall effectiveness in promoting his name and continued relevance in the world – and moreover, a world which is currently obsessed with the whole notion of the 'celebrity icon'. For this reason, I believe it could be useful to consider Jesus under three broad headings: 'Jesus by description', 'Jesus by definition', and 'Jesus by deduction'.

Jesus by description

Our primary source of information is the New Testament, which is a compilation of 27 individual writings. These comprise four Gospels, attributed to St Matthew, St Mark, St Luke and St John, which provide an account of Jesus' life, followed by the Acts, which describe the spread of the Christian movement, and a selection of Letters to individuals and emerging church communities that explain and expand upon the Gospels. The New Testament is a sequel to, and in our faith system the fulfilment of, the Old Testament, which is composed of a further 46 writings or books that begin with the story of creation and trace the continuing relationship or 'covenant' between God and the people of Israel.

Most Catholics will have a passing knowledge of these writings as a result of their use at Sunday Mass, but Scripture has never been our strong suit in the same way as it is with many other Christian Churches. Traditionally in Catholicism, the Bible was treated as a technical manual from which we were collectively taught by those 'suitably qualified' to do so, rather than it being promoted as a facility in which we should immerse ourselves as individuals. As a result, Catholics tend not to engage in serious biblical debate or make extensive use of specified quotes to support or refute a particular point of view. For the most part, we simply do not know enough quotes well enough to pursue this approach.

In truth, I suspect that many Catholics have never stopped to consider the subject matter of the Bible properly at all. We take its existence for granted, and we refer to it as the 'Word of God', but what does this actually mean? How did it become translated into the written format we now use? When and how was it put together, and by whom?

One of the consequences of this shallow awareness is that people can tend to regard the Gospels as being in the nature of a biography of Jesus, as if the evangelists were the equivalent of today's accredited Middle East correspondents for a news organisation. Each event or saying of Jesus is treated as an actual description of what occurred, or as a word-for-word account of what he said at the time, all presented in strict chronological order. In reality, there are several underlying factors involved here.

Timing

The first Gospel to appear is generally attributed to St Mark, written around 40 years after the death of Jesus, with the Gospel of St John not being completed until early in the second century AD. There were actually letters of St Paul which had come into circulation before any of the Gospels, but the significance in all these cases is that the written word was based on original eyewitness accounts as remembered by people at the time and passed on verbally during the intervening years.

To put this in context, a similar period of around 40 years has elapsed since the end of Vatican II. For this event we are able to access volumes of 'live time' reports, commentaries and newsreel footage to establish a clear picture of who said what and why.

41

And yet questions continue to arise in respect of individual issues, or at least the intentions behind some of the published texts. It is interesting to speculate what we would now be reading about the Council if written summaries were only just beginning to appear for the first time, based on original verbal testimonies of those who had been present and with the vast majority of these participants now deceased.

Sentiment

When the Gospels came to be written it was with the knowledge and a collective belief in the resurrection. Inevitably this will have coloured the way the early disciples remembered the original events and sayings from Jesus' life, and the way they came to view the whole episode of his passion and death. In other words, with the benefit of hindsight the Gospels became an expression of what the early Christians had come to believe about Jesus. This is not in any way to doubt the truth of their content, but merely to emphasise that they cannot be read as a factual and time-specific account of each event.

The Pontifical Biblical Commission issued an instruction on just this point as far back as 1964, entitled 'The Historical Truth of the Gospels'.[2] This made it clear that we do not have in the written Gospels the words and deeds of Jesus as exactly and completely as when first spoken or performed, nor do we have an accurate record of what was communicated verbally in the period following the resurrection and during the composition of the Gospels. What we have is the finally edited versions given to us by the evangelists.[3]

The Gospels therefore need to be understood as the inspired product of the 'Spirit' working in the minds of the people who reflected on the life of Jesus and his place in the evolving life of

---

[2] Referred to by Burns in *Roman Catholicism after Vatican II*, p. 6.
[3] ibid., p. 20.

the Christian communities. They also incorporate the individual interpretation and emphasis that the editors of the Gospels used in order to present Jesus in a particular light. For example, the focus of St Matthew was towards a traditional Jewish audience and so incorporates more references to Old Testament prophecies which he saw as being fulfilled in Jesus, whereas St John's account shows a markedly different style and approach from the three others and has been described as 'an old man's reflections on past events, delving into their deeper meaning … a very personal statement of faith in Christ'.[4]

Language

We need to consider the form and style of writing in the Bible, and distinguish in the text between the literal and the figurative, the use of myth, sign, symbol and allegory viewed in the context of the Jewish culture of the time. Today 'myth' conjures up the picture of make-believe, but Michael Morwood explains that this can be misleading, because in reality it is the endeavour of human beings to plumb the depths of mystery to find insights into the deepest questions of life's meaning and purpose. Beyond the story, beyond the 'symbol', people are trying to express insights and derive meaning and direction for personal and communal life from the mystical story.[5]

In other words, myths contain truths and insights that give meaning to who we are, and they have the ability to touch us at the deeper levels of meaning and purpose. They are misunderstood and wrongly used when people do not move beyond their literal sense and merely take each story to be factual. At that point the Bible can become a dangerous document, as history all too sadly records, when people argue and seek to enforce their wholly literal interpretations on others.

---

[4] *Your Faith* (Redemptorist Publications, 1990), p. 37.
[5] Morwood, *Tomorrow's Catholic*, p. 29.

Many Catholics may well find this information disturbing in view of what they had previously understood to be the form and nature of the New Testament, and in my view a comprehensive educational programme to explain the whole Gospel tradition is long overdue. I am not suggesting that everyone be forced to take a degree course in Bible Studies, but given the place which is rightly accredited to Scripture in our faith system, I consider that a properly planned instruction programme to supplement the readings at Sunday Mass could be of immeasurable advantage, compared to relying on 'ad hoc' homilies.

Our relative lack of biblical appreciation came into practical focus a few years ago with the publication of the novel *The Da Vinci Code*,[6] together with the film of the same name. Within a passably believable and certainly entertaining series of supposed historical events supported by mathematical 'evidence' was the claim that the Church had deliberately discarded a further Gospel account and suppressed information concerning a relationship between Jesus and Mary Magdalene. In no time at all a phalanx of books and pamphlets appeared from 'authorised experts' within the Church refuting claims of any physical relationship on the part of Jesus and denying that any special role had been intended for, let alone offered to, Mary Magdalene. What a pity that such informed biblical opinion had to wait for expression until prompted by what had been openly marketed as a commercial work of fiction.

It is also worth noting that the speed and the level of response by Church authorities, which even extended to calls by the Vatican for Catholics to boycott the film, gave fuel to the old adage that there is never smoke without fire. After all, this is a generation that thrives on conspiracy theories! On a more positive note, *The Da Vinci Code* did provide an opportunity to discuss religion in general and Catholicism in particular, but sadly I suspect that the episode may only have further exposed the limited knowledge of many Catholics concerning the Bible and their own Church history.

---

[6] Dan Brown, *The Da Vinci Code* (Bantam Press, 2003).

In my experience there are two issues which follow as a direct result of this situation. First, there are large numbers of us who grew up with a predominantly literal understanding of Gospel events, and the realisation that this is not the intended approach and that our pastoral leadership has always been aware of this can become a potential cause for disillusionment and even anger. 'Why', we may well ask, 'could we not have been treated as intelligent adults and been given a better explanation based on the fruits of biblical scholarship?' Moreover, when this realisation follows as a result of information or explanations that emanate from sources outside the Church – which is increasingly likely in our internet age – this can prompt some people to reach the conclusion that they have been 'duped' for too long and they simply vote with their feet.

A second issue is that without a better understanding of how post-resurrection influences may have determined the composition of the Gospels and the choice of language used by the individual authors, it is highly probable that the 'divine Jesus' will be the principal or even the sole image which comes across. As an example, in St Luke's account of the annunciation, Jesus is referred to as 'Son of the Most High', a clear reference to the God of Israel which conditions us right from the outset for the events that are to follow. A heavenly host arrives to greet Jesus' birth; the Magi travel to pay homage to a king; Jesus is described as having an encyclopedic understanding of the Scriptures at an early age; he is continuously reported as being able to know or second-guess the tricks and traps set by the Pharisees; and he performs miracles.

As indicated in the previous chapter, the focal symbol for Jesus' activity and teaching was to announce the kingdom of God, but if he is effectively thought of as a divine personage commissioned to undertake an assignment on earth, there is the risk that the impact of his message will be diminished. We could easily interpret what he said and did as predictable and easy for him given his origin and background, but as an altogether different matter for us who have to struggle through life as ordinary human beings.

Almost two thousand years later, we may also lose sight of the full human dimension which was present in God's unfolding plan. For example, we read the account of the annunciation when Mary was told she was to conceive the Son of God, to which she is recorded as giving her instant consent: 'Let what you have said be done to me' (Luke 1:38). But here was a young Jewish girl whose upbringing at that time would have made it unimaginable for her to countenance any connection between the divine and the human, let alone on this intimate level. It is easy to overlook what must have been her inner reaction to this extraordinary proposition and her thoughts on the whole drama that was to follow – including her need to find the right moment to inform her parents of the situation and then attempt to find the right words to explain the circumstances of her pregnancy.

The story of the annunciation is the account of an amazing girl, who had amazing parents and an amazing spouse in the person of Joseph. There is so much here that we can reflect upon in terms of the obvious doubts, anguish, soul-searching and possibly even arguments which may have taken place amongst those directly involved, but without deterring their resolve to see through what they came to believe as God's purpose. This is the real holy family, an inspiring and enduring example for us rather than the picture-postcard model that is frequently portrayed of Jesus, Mary and Joseph at a single point in history.

On a similar human theme, I remember some years ago reading a book entitled *Jesus, the Man who Lives*,[7] which was written by Malcolm Muggeridge, a well-known television personality at the time and for a large part of his life an avowed atheist. He set out to describe the event in a contemporary setting, suggesting that it would not have been long before Mary's friends and acquaintances in Nazareth became aware of her pregnancy, but with our less narrow-minded attitudes today, there would have been no social stigma attaching to her or her family. An unmarried teenage pregnancy

---

[7] Malcolm Muggeridge, *Jesus, the Man who Lives* (William Collins, 1975).

would, of course, be treated as yet another statistic to highlight the failure of the government's birth control programme and, given the prospective mother's continuous denial of any physical complicity, a psychological screening would almost certainly be organised by the local Social Services Department. Under these particular circumstances there would also be a strong probability of pressure being exerted on Mary to consider terminating her pregnancy, and as Muggeridge concludes, this may well signal that God's plan of salvation might simply not be permitted in our 'enlightened' age.

With the availability of modern techniques for biblical research, it is now possible to identify a basic historical foundation for Jesus' life and public ministry (historical criticism). We also have the ability to analyse the second stage of the Gospel tradition involving the verbal proclamation of the apostles and disciples (form criticism). The most recent area of development, which only dates from the middle of the twentieth century, now enables scholars to discover the dominant ideas which governed the final writing and editing of the Gospels to suit the particular theological and catechetical intentions of the authors (redaction criticism).[8]

In the final analysis, however, we cannot know the 'real' Jesus through historical research, but as Robert Burns says, we can know the Jesus of history whom we can recover and examine by using the scientific tools available to us.[9] In my view, we deserve to be better informed on the progress which continues to be made in this and allied fields, to add to our awareness and appreciation of the person of Jesus and his life amongst us.

Jesus by definition

The story of the resurrection of Jesus will always prompt questions concerning his origins and the nature and purpose of his earthly

---

[8] Referred to by Burns, *Roman Catholicism after Vatican II*, p. 7.
[9] ibid., p. 38.

presence. Many early 'Jewish Christians' found it difficult to identify even the exalted post-resurrection Jesus with God. For them, Jesus stands at the right side of the throne of God, in glory, in total communion with God, 'as a human being, the human representative before God'.[10]

In contrast, there were others for whom an acceptance of the God-man dimension of Jesus was less of a problem and, as recorded in the *Encyclopedia*, they began to pray to him and worship him 'in the power of the Spirit'.[11] As time progressed it became evident that there was a need to develop a consistent understanding of Jesus 'in himself' (Christology) that continued to retain its established Jewish roots but was capable of being communicated across ever-widening geographic and cultural lines. A doctrine was needed to answer questions such as these: Who is Jesus relative to God? How, within a monotheistic (one God) framework, can Jesus be the divine Saviour? Is he fully human with a human soul, and if so, how did he accomplish our salvation?

A challenge for Christianity during these early centuries came from a movement known as Gnosticism, a name derived from the Greek word for 'knowledge'. As a way of interpreting reality, Gnosticism was a dualistic philosophy which divided human experience into a good and real realm of spirit or a bad and illusory realm of matter and held that these two realms came from different sources which were always at enmity with one another. It was also an elitist philosophy whereby those with 'spiritual knowledge', i.e. the Gnostics, would be saved by escaping from the body and material constraints, some others might be helped to achieve a similar release, but for the majority of humanity there was no possible hope of salvation.[12]

These teachings on the dichotomy between the two assumed realms of existence was firmly refuted by St Irenaeus, who stressed that God alone was the sole Creator of everything that existed

---

[10] Morwood in *Tomorrow's Catholic*, p. 60.
[11] *Modern Catholic Encylopedia*, p. 451.
[12] ibid., p. 347.

and that all of creation had been seen at the outset to be good (Genesis 1:10). The fact that God's own Son Jesus was willing to become human was offered as further proof of the goodness of creation: Jesus recapitulated the career of Adam, going over the story of human sin but this time emerging triumphant – and for the sake of the whole of humanity, not just a selected few.[13]

A lively interest and debate on the 'status' of Jesus nevertheless continued unabated. Writing in the fourth century, Gregory of Nyssa reported that one could not go into the marketplace without getting involved in a discussion about whether God the Son is subordinate to God the Father, begotten or unbegotten, created from nothing (*ex nihilo*) or an ordinary man. Gregory questioned whether this enthusiasm for 'divine things' was a result of some intellectual derangement, but in the background at this time was an Egyptian priest named Arius whose teaching along Gnostic lines had begun to widen existing divisions within the Church.

Arius (AD 256–336) held that God (the Father) is absolutely unique and transcendent and that God's essence cannot be shared by another or transferred to another,(such as the Son) as this could imply a division in God. His contention was that Christ was begotten of God in time not from all eternity and as part of creation, Christ is inferior to God but greater than other creatures.[14] Arius offered biblical support for his case,[15] arguing that God could not take on human form which constitutes matter and is therefore from the realm of the bad.

At the behest of the Emperor Constantine, the bishops of the Church travelled to the town of Nicea (in modern-day Turkey) in order to examine and resolve these conflicting views. This was the first gathering of bishops to become officially designated as an 'Ecumenical Council', taken from the Greek word *oikumene*, meaning 'the whole of the known world'. It was effectively a formally convened meeting of bishops as representatives of the

---

[13] ibid., p. 436.
[14] Referred to by LaCugna in *The Trinitarian Mystery of God*, p. 165.
[15] See John 14:28; Colossians 1:6; Hebrews 1:2.

whole Church for the purpose of discussing and settling matters of concern for the whole Church.

The first four Ecumenical Councils defined Christian teaching in respect of the person of Jesus and can be summarised briefly as follows.

Nicea (AD 325)

To refute the claims by Arius of a diminished notion of Jesus' divinity as the Son of God, the Council asserted that Jesus is of one substance or being with God the Father, not simply of a similar substance and not created at a particular point in time but eternally begotten of the Father. This upheld the divinity of Jesus and the absolute unity between the Father and Jesus as the means whereby the eternal God had personally entered into the historical condition of humanity in Jesus of Nazareth.

The pivotal word to produce the definition was the Greek *homoousios*, meaning 'of the same being' (in Latin, *consubstantialis*), although for several reasons it did not secure the unanimous support of the Council Fathers. First, it was not a biblical term and some of the bishops considered that its use was inappropriate for the specific purpose of formulating doctrine. Second, the word itself is capable of different interpretations and it might, for example, be taken to imply that both Father and Son were the same person but operating in different guises at different times.

The Arian debate continued well after the close of the Council, but in upholding the divinity of Jesus and the mystery of God's incarnation in the person of Jesus, Nicea was significant for two reasons. As a divine personage, there could be no doubt that the life, death and resurrection of Jesus achieved its designed purpose; and for Jesus to assume a truly human nature and physical form puts to rest any claim that matter is intrinsically flawed.

Constantinople (AD 381)

At this second Ecumenical Council the bishops reconfirmed the 'one in being' of the Father and Son which had been agreed at Nicea, and then proceeded to expand on the earlier definition by incorporating a 'trinitarian' framework of Father, Son and Holy Spirit. The agreed text at the Council of Constantinople comprises the following statement:

> We believe in one God the Father all powerful, maker of heaven and of earth, and of all things both seen and unseen.
>
> And in one Lord Jesus Christ, the only- begotten Son of God, begotten from the Father before all the ages, light from light, true God from true God, begotten not made, consubstantial with the Father, through whom all things came to be;
>
> For us humans and for our salvation he came down from the heavens and became incarnate from the holy Spirit and the virgin Mary, became human and was crucified on our behalf by Pontius Pilate;
>
> He suffered and was buried and rose up on the third day in accordance with the scriptures; he is coming again with glory to judge the living and the dead; his kingdom will have no end.
>
> And in the Spirit, the holy, the lordly and life- giving one, proceeding forth from the Father, co-worshipped and glorified with the Father and Son, the one who spoke through the prophets;
>
> In one, holy, catholic and apostolic church.
>
> We confess one baptism for the forgiving of sins.
>
> We look forward to a resurrection of the dead and life in the age to come. Amen.[16]

---

[16] Referred to by Norman P. Tanner in *The Councils of the Church: A Short History* (Crossroad Publishing, 2001), p. 23.

It is immediately apparent that the Credo which we recite at Mass each Sunday is virtually identical to the text agreed at Constantinople – which, as the theologian and historian Norman Tanner comments, is a remarkable tribute to these early councils.[17]

Ephesus (AD 431)

The third Ecumenical Council was called to reject the claim that there were two separate persons in Jesus, one divine and the other human. This view had arisen as a result of the refusal by Nestorius, then bishop of Constantinople, to describe Mary as 'Mother of God' (*theotokos*) or 'God bearer', claiming that she had only given birth to a man in whom God dwelt. The Council of Ephesus affirmed the unity of Jesus by recognising Mary's title and a 'Formula of Union' was later agreed to confirm that Jesus was one person with two natures – one divine and one human.

Chalcedon (AD 451)

As at Nicea a century before, the decision reached by the bishops at Ephesus did not totally eliminate ongoing disputes or prevent new propositions being introduced. One such formulation was that Jesus had two natures before but only one nature after the incarnation – a position known as Monophysitism (from the Greek *mono* = 'one'; *physis* = 'nature').

This proposition was rejected by the Council, which proclaimed that there were two distinct natures that were united in the person of the 'God-man' Jesus. It then became the task of the assembled bishops to formulate the manner in which the divine and human natures were combined, drawing together the teachings of the previous councils that Jesus is truly God and truly man, begotten before the ages from the Father in his divinity and from Mary

---

[17] ibid., p. 25.

the God-bearer as regards his humanity. By formal definition at Chalcedon, Jesus was acknowledged as having two natures which:

> undergo no confusion, no change, no division, no separation; at no point was the difference between natures taken away through the union but rather the property of both natures is preserved and comes together into a single person and as a single subsistent being; he is not parted or divided into two persons but is the one and the same only begotten Son, God, Word, Lord Jesus Christ, just as the prophets taught from the beginning about him and as the Lord Jesus Christ himself instructed us, and as the creed of the fathers handed it down to us.[18]

In this formulation the Council of Chalcedon defined the 'Hypostatic Union' (from the Greek *hypostasis*, meaning 'individual' or 'person'), the union of two distinct natures of God and man in the person of Jesus, who is true God and true man.[19] One wonders how many Catholics today have ever heard of this expression, let alone appreciate its significance when seeking to understand how Jesus fulfils the titles and descriptions which we are inclined to attribute to him with little further thought.

It is important also to remember that what we now accept as fundamental doctrine concerning Jesus was not simply 'known' within the Church. Under the guidance of the Spirit it took several centuries for this to evolve into clear formulations as a result of considerable reflection, debate and prayer.

Jesus by deduction

To summarise the story so far, we have identified the 'Jesus of history', who led a comparatively short but active public life as

---

[18] ibid., p. 28.
[19] *Modern Catholic Encylopedia*, p. 411.

an inspiring preacher giving encouragement and hope particularly to the marginalised in society. Along the way he managed to upset the religious and civil establishment of the time, which resulted in his eventual arrest, trial and crucifixion. Not surprisingly, his death caused many of his original followers to lose heart, but word began to circulate based on the first-hand testimonies of some of his closest disciples that they had again met and spoken with him. Jesus had been raised from the dead.

The 'Jesus of faith' became a reality as news of his resurrection began to spread. In the words of Robert Burns, the one who proclaimed the kingdom of God in his own lifetime became after his death and resurrection the one proclaimed.[20] As time progressed, the way that Jesus was remembered became increasingly coloured by the post-resurrection enthusiasm experienced within many of the early Christian communities and could sometimes admit to exaggerations, misinterpretations and even misrepresentations. A universal code became necessary to identify and establish 'orthodoxy' (right teaching) as opposed to 'heterodoxy' (wrong teaching), and this set the agenda for a series of General or Ecumenical Councils to establish a definitive doctrine concerning Jesus.

Taken together, the findings of these Councils represent the unique claim of the Christian faith that Jesus is truly God and at the same time truly human. We have, of course, heard this many times – but what does it actually mean? How do we understand the Jesus of history and the Jesus of faith in today's Church? People are likely to have their own mental picture of Jesus courtesy of the numerous Hollywood and television films on the subject, and this may well be the image which we project when listening to Sunday Gospel readings. But is this enough to deepen our understanding of the person of Jesus and help us to understand what our relationship with him is really about?

The 1994 *Catechism* informs us that the name 'Jesus' means in Hebrew 'God saves' and that this expresses his identity and

---

[20] Burns, *Roman Catholicism after Vatican II*, p. 12.

his mission (#430). The word 'Christ', from the Greek translation of the Hebrew *Messiah*, means 'anointed one', which becomes the name proper to Jesus because he accomplished perfectly the divine mission that 'Christ' signifies (#436).

At his baptism and transfiguration, reference is made to the announcement by God that Jesus is his 'Blessed Son', and that when used by him as a title, it affirms his eternal pre-existence (#444). Based on the Hebrew name used by God to reveal himself to Moses, the Greek translation is given as *Kyrios*, or 'Lord', and is stated to indicate the divinity of Israel's God. In the Gospels it relates to both the Father and Jesus, who is thereby recognised as God himself (#446).

We have now identified the full doctrinal title 'Lord Jesus Christ, Son of God'. However, the initial impression which these several definitions and accompanying descriptions convey to me is that Jesus could have been a divine visitor to earth who took on a human form in order to carry out a predetermined mission on which he had been fully briefed at the outset. On its successful completion we could simply assume that he returned to heaven.

The *Catechism* later confirms in Chalcedon-type language that Jesus was truly human while remaining truly divine (#464), but I suspect that by this stage in the reading many people will already have formed an opinion of God acting out an event in history under the guise of a human appearance. Reference is also made to Jesus enjoying in his human knowledge *the fullness* (my emphasis) of the eternal plan he had come to reveal (#474), which only seems to reinforce the notion of Jesus as a human 'front', or at the very least as being substantively different from the rest of us.

This 'top down' approach, as it came to be described, with a particular emphasis on the divinity of Jesus, was the prevalent viewpoint amongst theologians in the Church up to the middle of the twentieth century.[21] With it comes the risk that Jesus' humanity

---

[21] A description attributed to Karl Rahner in 1971, and referred to by Burns in *Roman Catholicism after Vatican II*, p. 20.

might be treated as superficial, or at best be seen to be incidental to the main plot. And yet Vatican II speaks of Jesus working with human hands, thinking with a human mind, acting with a human will and loving with a human heart, 'fully revealing humanity to itself'.[22] There seems to be an element of inconsistency here.

A second observation on the *Catechism* account is that it provides little to help us know Jesus in the sense of our affinity with him as a fellow human being. We are simply given his names and titles with a description of what these are intended to signify, whereas when we speak of 'knowing' someone this generally means more than being able to quote their date of birth, present address and what they do for a living. Knowing someone is to become increasingly aware of what makes them tick as a person and how this is likely to influence the way they act or react to particular situations.

Contrast the description of Jesus given by Karen Kilby: 'If being orientated towards God is what makes us human, then the one who is so orientated that he is utterly given over to God and utterly taken over by God is actually the one who is at the same time the most fully human.'[23] Jesus is this supreme example and in his openness to God, God's self-communication is met with a free and perfect response. Surely this is what the Fathers at Vatican II meant when they spoke of Jesus revealing humanity to itself.

A greater emphasis on the human aspect of Jesus, which can be termed a 'bottom up' approach, will therefore begin with the Jesus of history in the context of what it means for each of us to be human. Specifically, it will begin with our relatedness to God, in whose image and likeness we are created, and with the opportunity we have been given to participate in his life through the gifts of knowledge, freedom and love. As this is described by W. Dyche, human beings came to be so that God can share his life in this way. We were not simply created and left to get on with life with God's self-revelation (grace) hovering above us as

---

[22] 'Pastoral Constitution on the Church in the Modern World' (*Gaudium et Spes*), #25.
[23] Kilby, *Karl Rahner*, p. 19.

an added embellishment, but rather this revelation was embedded within the deepest identity of humankind.[24]

To focus more on the human dimension of Jesus does not, in my view, detract from his divine nature and all that flows from this, but it can enable us to better appreciate our own inbuilt potential based on his inspiration, encouragement and track record as a fellow human being rather than as an 'external' role model. We can relate to Jesus as someone who genuinely knows all the trials and tribulations of the human condition, having experienced them in the same way as us. This is very well described by Robert Burns: 'In reaching out to Jesus, one is really reaching out to touch a brother but is at the same time being touched and embraced by God himself.'[25]

Jesus needs to be seen as the presence of God's saving activity in the world in such a way that he is part of the world, not an external deity breaking into human affairs. As considered in the last chapter, the purpose of the incarnation was not to change God's mind about us, or to turn his wrath to mercy, or through Jesus' death to persuade God to be gracious. The essential premise as described by Karen Kilby is that Jesus is not the trigger for God to become gracious, but the peak of God being gracious, a high point in the history of salvation rather than a turning point.[26]

A third observation on the *Catechism* account concerns what I regard as the lack of any real explanation of the genesis of Jesus of Nazareth. He is described as being truly divine and truly human, but without saying how this came about and how this was sustained during his earthly existence. In other words, where was Jesus before he became the Jesus of history, and where is the Jesus of history now, following his resurrection?

These and similar questions are not answered by simply parroting the statement that Jesus is the Son of God, or by repeating

---

[24] W. Dyche, 'Transcendental Theology' in *Karl Rahner* (Outstanding Christian Thinkers series), (Geoffrey Chapman, 1992), p. 72.
[25] Burns, *Roman Catholicism after Vatican II*, p. 23.
[26] Kilby, *Karl Rahner*, p. 27.

expressions such as 'pre-existing Word' or 'eternally begotten' which can be confusing or misleading without proper explanations. For example, referring to Jesus as the 'pre-existing Word' could be taken to imply that 'he' was always an entity in his own right alongside or distinct from God and, in the extreme, that his humanity could have existed in some fashion before the incarnation.

I am not suggesting that these expressions relating to Jesus are ignored or abandoned, but rather that we find a better way to communicate the truths that are held in these traditional formulations and express them in today's language. My generation was prepared to accept articles of faith as presented, but this no longer holds for younger Catholics who rightly call for fuller explanations to support the teachings which they are expected to follow in order to be satisfied of their relevance to everyday life. They will otherwise simply nod an approval without any real follow-up interest in the topic.

There must surely be an abundance of expertise within the Church which our pastoral leadership is able to marshal and charge with the task of presenting the Jesus of history and the Jesus of faith, adopting an approach and language which strike a chord with a generation who may not be wholly convinced of what is presently on offer. As my contribution to the process, I believe the areas which call for further guidance and clarification include the following.

How we think and speak about God

We describe Jesus as the Son of God, from which it is easy to form the image of an older male version with the full trappings of parental authority, who resides elsewhere but intervenes in our situation whenever this is regarded as appropriate. The risk here, as described by Karen Kilby, is that we come to regard God as an easy word to understand, just another concept we can pin down, one thing among many that we can talk about with equal facility.[27]

---

[27] ibid., p. 8.

In reality, God is never known in this way and can never be for us 'a member of the larger household of all reality'. We gain a glimpse of God through Jesus, but we need to acknowledge that we are unable to explain him fully, as our intellect and vocabulary are simply inadequate for the task.[28] To repeat the view expressed by St Thomas Aquinas, we know *that* God is, but not *what* God is, other than by his actions.

How we define our relationship with God, each other and creation

The Old Testament abounds with examples of God's actions throughout history as experienced by the people of Israel and speaks of divine activity being implemented through the agencies of 'Wisdom', 'Word' and 'Spirit'. As described by Gerald O'Collins, these personified instruments of divine activity were not formally recognised as persons, but operated with personal characteristics. In particular, Wisdom (Greek: *Sophia* – and also female!) was associated with all God's creative works and helped overcome a sense of divide between the transcendent otherness of God and the divine presence or immanence in creation.[29]

By the time of the New Testament, the title of Wisdom was being ascribed to Jesus, no doubt reflecting a belief that through his life, death and resurrection he had generated a 'new creation' of graced life for everyone (Romans 1:16). Jesus became recognised as one and the same divine agent for both 'original' and 'new' creation. In the words of St Paul, 'He [God] has let us know the mystery of his purpose, the hidden plan he so kindly made in Christ from the beginning ... and it is in him that we were claimed as God's own, chosen from the beginning' (Ephesians 1:9–11).

We can therefore see Jesus as an intrinsic element of God's

---

[28] ibid., p. 12.
[29] O'Collins, *Jesus our Redeemer*, p. 29.

being (eternally begotten) and when spoken of synonymously with Wisdom he can be clearly identified as the principal component in implementing creation. This, of course, is what we profess in our weekly Credo, that 'through him all things were made', but I wonder how many Catholics actually pick up on these words and appreciate the connectedness between creation and the incarnation.

It becomes apparent also that the Word/Wisdom/Son of God/Jesus is actually the prototype for humanity in that we are all created in this same image and likeness. The incarnation of Jesus was always part of the plan, irrespective of the actions of Adam and Eve, and is the event that defines our relationships – to God, to each other and to the rest of creation. Humanity understands itself in God's own light and finds its ultimate fulfilment in following a lifelong pilgrimage to reach the fullness of this goal.[30]

How we explain the incarnation

Against this backcloth, how do we explain the incarnation itself, the actual process whereby 'the Word became flesh and lived among us' (John 1:14)? In our twenty-first-century world, the 'credibility target' to satisfy contemporary expectations will be to seek to explain by what means an identifiable embryo took form in a human womb with the same physiological composition as any other human embryo, but in this case without any involvement by a human father. We know from today's medical science that to be a human person, Jesus will have been born with his own DNA profile – his unique 'human genome' – of 46 individual chromosomes, of which half will have been inherited from his mother. But what about the remainder?

We need to admit that there is no simple answer here, and no means by which we can supply irrefutable genetic evidence that can be submitted for proper scientific investigation. The Jesus of

---

[30] ibid., p. 25.

history is a matter of record, but there is no seamless route between this and the Jesus of faith, who remains just that – a matter of faith. At least there is a consistency and a resonance here in Christian belief that, beginning with the 'Big Bang', everything has come about and is sustained because God wills it to be so – that such a cosmic order suggests an ultimate sufficient reason: a cosmic Orderer.[31]

How we understand the divinity and humanity of Jesus

If we are willing for the moment to accept the Christian claim that Jesus is both divine and human, it becomes important to give further thought to the way in which we describe and understand his second nature, since by necessity this has a direct bearing on us as fellow human beings. So, for example, if we judge human nature as being wholly definable, something that can be set within boundaries and specified exactly, nothing more than a product of 46 chromosomes, it is not at all clear how an infinite and omniscient God could become something so circumscribed and delimited and yet still in any sense be God.[32]

Alternatively, if we revisit and follow the theology of Karl Rahner concerning our relatedness to God (see Chapter 1), human nature is seen not to be closed in on itself but instinctively able to consider meaning, values and purpose; to comprise a kind of infinite openness which is always striving beyond the finite to that which is beyond the world, to what Rahner refers to as a holy mystery – to God. In Rahner's view, 'when we have said everything about ourselves that can be described and defined we have still said nothing about ourselves unless we have included or implied the fact that we are beings that are referred to the incomprehensible God'.[33]

On this basis, Jesus can be understood not as a hybrid, or as

---

[31] ibid., p. 26.
[32] Kilby, *Karl Rahner*, p. 19.
[33] ibid.

God simply adopting a human disguise, but as what it really is to be human. As this is described by Karen Kilby, the divinity of Jesus is something which on the one hand belongs only to him – something unique and absolute – but on the other hand can be situated within the much broader phenomenon of the common humanity of us all, the extreme case of what it is to be human, like us only more so, what we are if we take it all the way to its limit.[34] What a boost this is for our individual self-esteem, as well as being a reminder of the responsibilities which we owe to each other.

How we explain the way Jesus functioned as both divine and human

This brings us to the question of how Jesus functioned, being both divine and human. We are frequently reminded that he was like us in all things except sin, but does this mean that Jesus could not sin or did not sin?

As the pre-existing Word the issue does not arise, but his human nature will have included the same freedom as we have to make decisions and therefore the same propensity to sin – witness the efforts made by the devil to tempt him in the desert (Matthew 4:1–11). The reason why Jesus did not succumb to these or any other temptations must therefore reflect the measure of his orientation towards God and his total obedience which sprang from this.

The *Catechism* states that Jesus was fully aware of God's eternal plan (#474), but does not explain when and how this awareness came about. One school of thought is that because of the hypostatic union of the divine and the human nature in Jesus he was not in any way limited in knowledge, but if this was the case it represents a second difference between him and us and reopens the question of why the devil would waste time in trying to tempt him in the first place.

---

[34] ibid., p. 20.

An alternative view is that Jesus had an intuitive knowledge or awareness of who he was, but that he had to acquire the ability to express this to himself and then to others gradually over time.[35] This seems more consistent with the view of St Paul that although Jesus' state was divine, he did not cling to his equality with God, but emptied himself to assume the condition of a slave and became as men are (Philippians 2:6–7).

I feel more comfortable with this explanation for Jesus' self-knowledge where the key concept is that he emptied himself (the Greek word is *kenosis*) of his divine insights. As this is described by Robert Burns, Jesus emptied himself from a condition in which divine attributes, including omniscience, were fully operative, to a state in which he took on a fully human nature. And yet from the very beginning of his earthly life he was indeed divine as well as human, and therein lies the mystery of the incarnation.[36]

How we explain the Jesus of history

A further point which I consider calls for greater clarity is how we should attempt to explain the Jesus of history following his resurrection. In the words of St Paul, if Jesus had not been raised from the dead our faith would have been in vain and we would still be in our sins (1 Corinthians 15:17–18). That is the theology, but what did the event actually entail?

There is evidence of a physical aspect to Jesus from his birth through to his death on the cross and the clear message of the New Testament is that something also happened to this same Jesus thereafter. God raised him from death, as opposed to merely providing some form of reassurance to his disciples. He was alive again and the evangelists speak of a risen Jesus in terms of touching (Luke 24:39), eating (Luke 24:41–43) and conversing (John 21:15–22). All these are physical manifestations.

---

[35] Burns, *Roman Catholicism after Vatican II*, p. 22.
[36] ibid., p. 21.

By contrast, there are other references to Jesus 'coming and going' in a manner unlike a mortal body (Luke 24:31), or appearing in 'another form' (Mark 16:12), or standing before his disciples but they were unable to recognise him (Luke 24:16). So what was the actual 'bodiliness' of Jesus following the resurrection? In the words of Robert Burns, the resurrection cannot be viewed simply as the resuscitation of a dead body. Something radically different had occurred.[37]

In his first letter to the Corinthians, St Paul makes the distinction between Jesus' physical body during his life and his spiritual body after the resurrection, but he emphasises that there is a continuity between the person who was and the person who will be. For this purpose he uses the analogy of the relation between the 'body' of the seed and the 'body' of the plant – an analogy of continuity but also of difference between different bodies (1 Corinthians 15:35–49).

This is expanded upon by Robert Burns, who explains that the Christian claim concerning the resurrection of Jesus is not that he returned to his former manner of living, but rather that after his death he entered into an entirely new form of existence, one in which he shared his power as God with others. The resurrection experience is not simply something that happened to Jesus; it is something that was shared by his followers, a new life through the power of the Holy Spirit.[38]

In summary, I believe there is a serious need to improve the general level of understanding and appreciation of Scripture within the Church, as well as to promote a greater awareness of later doctrinal formulations concerning the person of Jesus. Without this there will continue to be a tendency to depersonalise Jesus, for him to be thought of purely as a symbol of God's presence rather than as the physical manifestation of God's involvement in human history. As observed by Karl Rahner, many Catholics are

---

[37] ibid., p. 10.
[38] ibid., p. 11.

effectively 'closet Docetists' in that they view the incarnation as an essentially divine intervention – God appearing in human clothing in order to make himself visible in the world.[39]

Such a view deprives them of the whole theology of Jesus as a person who is not outside our reach but is a fellow human being who thereby gives proper meaning to the concept of our being created in the image and likeness of God (Genesis 1:26). This is a concept that defines us in terms of our relationship to God and our ongoing dialogue with God, whom we would subsequently be encouraged by Jesus to refer to as *Abba*, 'Father'.

In the early years of the Church, 'image' was seen to be permanent, while 'likeness' became viewed as the image in action and therefore liable to change – to progress or regress or even disappear through sin. As described by Gerald O'Collins, whatever human beings are as God's image, they are, and they cannot *not* be, because if they were to cease to be God's image, they could no longer be human.[40]

The image of God is therefore at the very heart of human existence and as such, I consider that we require more guidance in this area from our pastoral leadership. We need to be helped to recapture the essence of the Church's earlier theology of our image being a call through Jesus to participate in God's own being. As a religious mystery this will invite a lifetime of reflection and we can never expect to argue everything out in complete and final detail, but this is surely no excuse in the meantime for inadequate or inaccurate exegesis.[41]

---

[39] Referred to by Kilby, *Karl Rahner*, p. 18. Docetism is a heresy holding that Jesus was not really human, but only seemed to have a human body and was therefore illusory.
[40] O'Collins, *Jesus our Redeemer*, p. 25.
[41] ibid., p. ix.

4

And the Spirit Makes Three

In the name of the Father and of the Son and of the Holy
Spirit.
Amen.

This is the salutation with which we begin and end our prayers
and which we usually accompany by making the sign of the cross.
Its familiarity probably means that little thought is given to the
why or the how of the interrelationship(s) to which it refers.

I was formally introduced to this 'third element' in the run-
up to my Confirmation, which in those days closely followed
one's first Confession and first Holy Communion, depending on
the bishop's schedule for parish visits. The name used at the time
alternated between Holy Ghost and Holy Spirit, with the former
usually registering a higher novelty rating amongst that age group.

I still have my preparation book for Confirmation, entitled
Come O Holy Spirit.[1] This informs that the Spirit was active at
the birth of the world, the birth of Jesus and the birth of the
Church and was present at the birth of grace in our souls. Each
of these instances is supported by relevant passages from the
Scriptures, and the Spirit is depicted interchangeably in the form
of a wind, a breath, a flame or a dove.

Not surprisingly, the particular activity of the Spirit which
received most attention for the purpose of the sacrament of

---

[1] *Come O Holy Spirit* (Catholic Truth Society, 1950), by a Sister of Notre Dame.

Confirmation was when Our Lady and the apostles were present in the upper room in Jerusalem and suddenly:

> They heard what sounded like a powerful wind from heaven, the noise of which filled the entire house in which they were sitting; and something appeared to them that seemed like tongues of fire; these separated and came to rest on the heads of each of them. They were all filled with the Holy Spirit and began to speak foreign languages as the Spirit gave them the gift of speech. (Acts 2:2–4)

Before this event, the apostles were described as being weak in their faith, but this now became strong, such that it could not be shaken. Full of grace and zeal, they left the upper room and went into the marketplace to preach about Jesus. The change which had been effected in the apostles was the promise of what was in prospect for each of us through the sacrament of Confirmation. The entry of the Spirit would make us strong and perfect Christians and would clothe us in spiritual armour to become soldiers of Jesus. In this way we would be able to resist the three stated enemies of our souls, 'the devil, the world and the flesh'.[2]

Our preparatory instruction for the sacrament of Confirmation ran for a number of weeks and we were required to memorise several stock phrases, just in case we were asked questions by the bishop during the service. And so, in due course and in accord with due ritual, I became a confirmed Catholic at the age of nine, full in the knowledge of the following points:

1. There is one God comprising three persons: the Father, Son and Holy Spirit. The Son has two natures: one divine, the other human. The Spirit endows us with seven gifts which can translate into twelve life aids.[3]

---

[2] ibid., p. 28.
[3] The seven gifts of the Spirit are listed as Wisdom, Understanding, Counsel, Fortitude, Knowledge, Piety, Fear of the Lord. The twelve fruits are given as Charity, Joy, Peace, Patience, Benignity, Goodness, Longanimity, Mildness, Faith, Modesty, Continence, Chastity.

2. This 'three in one' composition is God's way of being
    and the way the Father generously chose to respond to
    an original human transgression and our continued poor
    behaviour. It was for Jesus to redeem our flawed condition
    by his death and resurrection with the cooperation of
    the Holy Spirit.
3. Before his return to heaven, Jesus instructed his closest
    followers on how to preserve and promote his message.
    Their appointment, which came with full delegated
    powers, was endorsed by the Spirit and this same mandate
    continues today in the form of the Church.

Fifty-plus years later, I remain a confirmed member of the self-
same Church, although I have to admit that for much of this
period I have not devoted a great deal of time or effort to try
to better understand the nature and workings of the Spirit. It
follows from this that my appreciation of the Trinity – 'the unity'
of Father, Son and Holy Spirit – is even more peripheral and
prompts me to ask, (a) whether I am unusual in this regard, and
(b) if not, whether this should be a cause for concern.

In answer to the first part of the question, I do not consider
myself untypical. There is a general awareness of the Trinity within
the Church, but I suspect that for the most part this is based on
little more than the use of the salutation mentioned above. Beyond
this we are reminded from time to time in Sunday homilies that
the Spirit perpetually guides the Church and can be a source of
enlightenment in our individual lives, but from my recollections
this has seldom been accompanied by any real explanation of
what it is and why it operates in this way.

'Father' and 'Son' are, of course, readily understandable labels
from everyday experience, whereas 'Spirit' is a less tangible
designation and when considered alongside the former can seem
to be an entity that functions in its own right and operates with
its own agenda. The situation is not helped by describing each
of the three elements of the Trinity as 'persons' and is perhaps a

further example of how the unqualified or unexplained use of words can serve to confuse rather than enthuse.

For example, in today's parlance, the word 'person' is likely to convey the understanding of an individual conscious subject, so what might seem to be presented here is the concept of three 'individual centres of consciousness' which collectively constitute the one single being. At face value this begins to have the feel of an abstract theory which, as Karl Rahner put it, has become irrelevant for practical piety – a Christian add-on to what might otherwise be a generally acceptable doctrine of God.[4]

And yet the Trinity is held to be a central tenet of our faith, so I believe that a diminished appreciation of the role of the Spirit and the doctrine of the Trinity must be a cause for concern. Colin Gunton has said that if we wish to understand how God works in our world, we should follow the route he has given us – the incarnation of his Son and the life-giving actions of his Spirit.[5] The doctrine of the Trinity allows us a glimpse of the God who meets us in Jesus through the Spirit.

The Spirit in Scripture and tradition

The biblical origins of the 'Spirit' can be traced back to the Hebrew word *ruah*, meaning 'wind' or 'breath' and indicating one of the personified agents of divine activity mentioned in the previous chapter. The 'curriculum vitae' for the Spirit will therefore include roles such as the creative breath which hovered over the waters (Genesis 1:2), that breathed life into man (Genesis 2:7), that gave strength to the heroes of Israel (Samuel 11:6) and endowed its wise men with intellect (Judges 6:34).

The prophet Ezekiel expanded on this imagery of the power of the Spirit, which he described as returning the people of Israel

---

[4] Referred to by Colin Gunton in *Father, Son and Holy Spirit* (T. & T. Clark, 2003), p. 5.
[5] ibid., p. 11.

from the death of their exile (in Babylon) to a new life in their homeland: 'I will put my Spirit within you and you shall live' (Ezekiel 7:14). He also envisaged the Spirit of God being placed not just within a selected few, but within the entire people as an interior power to transform their hearts: 'I will give you a new heart and put a new spirit within you. I will put my spirit within you' (Ezekiel 36:26–27).

The New Testament begins with the Spirit overshadowing Mary to bring about the incarnation of Jesus, 'who will be holy and will be called Son of God' (Luke 1:35). Following his baptism in the Jordan at the beginning of his public ministry, the Holy Spirit descended upon Jesus in bodily shape like a dove and a voice came from heaven saying, 'You are my Son, the Beloved; my favour rests on you' (Luke 3:22).

For St Paul, the Holy Spirit was at the heart of Christian belief and life (Romans 8:1–15). In his view, life without the Spirit was no life at all, devoid of power, sweetness and hope, whereas the Spirit of life poured out by the risen Lord gives power to live in a totally different way. The Spirit unites believers so intimately with Jesus that in the Holy Spirit they have a whole new way to pray, addressing the first divine person with Jesus' own intimate, familiar name, *Abba* (Galatians 4:6).

St Paul also stressed that the activity of the Spirit did not form isolated individuals but a community of people in loving relationship, united to the triune God and to each other in a 'communion' (from the Greek word *koinonia*, meaning 'a sharing in common' or 'participation') of the Holy Spirit (2 Corinthians 13:14). Through the Spirit we are baptised into the one body of Christ, the Church, we drink of the one Spirit, and each of us is given his or her own gifts and service in fostering the growth of the entire body (1 Corinthians 12:4–11).

The early disciples of Jesus can be seen to have experienced an overwhelming new life within and among themselves, and they identified the source of this life as the same Spirit who permeated Jesus' human existence and in whose power he was raised from the dead.[6] These disciples, who were almost exclusively Jewish, had little difficulty believing that the God they worshipped through Jesus was the same as the God they had always worshipped. As Colin Gunton commented, 'They did not find a new God but a new and loving way of knowing Him.'[7]

The Spirit can therefore be seen from Scripture to have been active at the outset of creation and throughout God's ongoing relationship with humanity, reaching its high point in the resurrection of Jesus. The common thread in all of this is that the Spirit is synonymous with life, it is deeply embedded in the make-up of each of us and it bestows a special power. God makes the gift of his Spirit and by this gift the love of God – that which is in the heart of God – is poured into our hearts.[8]

The Trinity

There are several 'triadic' (three-component) texts in the New Testament, notably the command of Jesus to his apostles to make disciples of all the nations, baptising them 'in the name of the Father and of the Son and of the Holy Spirit' (Matthew 28:19). However, as observed by Catherine LaCugna, Scripture does not contain an explicit doctrine of the Trinity but under the guidance of the Spirit, its undeniable testimony would eventually become celebrated in the Church's liturgy and affirmed in future creeds.

The early Christian communities increasingly came to recognise that the traditional images of the Spirit – breath, wind, fire – merely hinted at the Spirit's real identity as a someone rather than a something – a someone who does not receive life as a creature does but rather gives life as only God can (John 6:63).[9]

---

[6] *Modern Catholic Encylopedia*, p. 393.
[7] Gunton, *Father, Son and Holy Spirit*, p. 6.
[8] Francis-Xavier Durrwell, *The Spirit of the Father and the Son* (St Paul Publications, 1990), p. 26.
[9] *Modern Catholic Encyclopedia*, p. 394.

In the second century, St Irenaeus famously spoke of God's creating and redeeming work being achieved through his two hands – the Son and the Spirit. The analogy may appear simplistic, but, as Colin Gunton has argued, it is actually extremely subtle. Our hands are essentially ourselves in action, so when we write a letter, type a script, paint a picture or extend a hand in friendship, we ourselves are actually doing it. In this image, then, Jesus and the Spirit are God in action, God's way of being and acting in the world.[10]

It seems evident from this example that a 'trinitarian outlook' had become a feature of Church life, but without there being a formalised doctrine as such. In other words, there was no specific teaching which would define in what sense Father, Son and Spirit are all God but still only one God, or which would explain who this God could be who identifies himself in such a distinctive and personal way.[11]

As described in the previous chapter, the Council of Nicea (AD 325) declared the divinity of Jesus, but simply stated a belief in the Holy Spirit. It took until the Council of Constantinople (AD 381) for the Church to formally affirm the divinity of the Spirit by adding the words already present in Scripture that the Spirit is 'the Lord and Giver of life' (see again John 6:63).[12]

The Arian controversy at that time demanded clear teaching on what the Father, Son and Spirit shared in common (divinity) and what differentiated them from each other (personhood). An acceptable formula which was able to address these issues called for the use of technical language, much of which was drawn from Hellenistic philosophy and included words such as *ousia* ('nature') and *hypostasis* ('relation of origin'). So in its classic form, the doctrine of the Trinity asserted that 'God is one nature, three persons'.[13]

---

[10] Gunton, *Father, Son and Holy Spirit*, p. 12.
[11] ibid., p. 11.
[12] Referred to by Tanner in *The Councils of the Church: A Short History*, p. 24.
[13] LaCugna, *The Trinitarian Mystery of God*, p. 168

This use of 'non-biblical' vocabulary can be said to have contributed to a change in the focus of theology, which began to move from questions about what God does (his function) to questions about what God is (the nature of his being). The history of the Trinity from the time of the Council of Constantinople onwards is also the history of a divergence of views between the Greek (Orthodox) Church of the East and the Latin (Roman Catholic) Church of the West.

As a generalisation, I believe it may be fair to say that the emphasis in Greek theology remains that of the divine persons (*hypostasis*) who collectively make up the one God, whereas Latin theology became more orientated towards a consideration of the divine nature of the one God (*ousia*) who was comprised of three persons. This may appear to be little more than 'splitting hairs', but as Catherine LaCugna explains, Greek trinitarian theology has a dynamic understanding of God which retains the biblical emphasis on God's actions in accord with his plan of salvation – in theological speak, the 'economy of salvation' ('economy' here being taken from the Greek word *oikonomia*, meaning 'plan' or 'administration'). Thus God the Father creates through Jesus in the power of the Holy Spirit, who leads us back to the Father through Jesus.[14]

This does not tell us precisely what God is or what the divine persons are, other than obliquely in terms of their origin, but, as LaCugna continues, 'The personal property of the Father, that which makes the Father unique is unbegottenness (coming from no one); the personal property of the Son is begottenness (coming from the Father); the personal property of the Spirit is procession (coming from the Father).' The unity of God can therefore be said to reside in the mutual interdependence of the three persons in each other, for which the definitional Greek term is *perichoresis* – in its literal translation a 'round dance' of the Trinity.[15]

Latin theology has tended to follow a slightly different path,

---

[14] ibid.
[15] ibid., p. 169.

with the general direction being set by St Augustine (d. AD 430), who developed a number of psychological type analogies based on the human soul. In this model, the one substance – the soul – which is a reflection of its Creator is seen to exist in distinct representations or operations (i.e. knowing and loving and being known and loved) without partitioning the substance and so supporting the argument that the one God exists in the generation of the Word and the procession of the Spirit.[16]

This approach clearly underlines the shared divinity of the three persons, but does tend to diminish the distinction between them, since each is defined only in relation to each other instead of in terms of a specific role in our salvation. Over time, this focus on the 'internal relationship' aspect of God developed into a subject in its own right, and the doctrine of the Trinity became the means by which to speculate about the nature of God but without reference to his activities as recorded in the Scriptures. In the words of Catherine LaCugna, 'For many people today, the term Trinity evokes some image of the internal self-relatedness of God rather than the life of God that permeates every moment and aspect of our existence.'[17]

Filioque

The divergence between the Churches of the East and the West comes into sharpest focus as a result of the doctrine of *filioque*. I suspect that few people have come across this Latin word (which translates as 'and the Son'), let alone realise its historical and indeed continuing impact on East-West Church relations.

The belief of the Church based on the teachings of the Councils at Nicea and Constantinople (see Chapter 3) affirmed that the Holy Spirit 'proceeds from the Father'. Several centuries later, the

---

[16] ibid., p. 170.
[17] ibid., p. 172.

Latin Church in the West added the extra detail, *filioque*, thereby proclaiming that the Holy Spirit proceeds 'from the Father *and* from the Son', which of course remains the version in use today in our Sunday Credo.

The additional word originated in Spain to counter various heresies denying the divinity of Jesus and appears to have been regarded by its advocates as a local adaptation for a specific need, not a change in doctrine. The *filioque* clause began to be used in Rome from the beginning of the eleventh century and became officially sanctioned by the Fourth Lateran Council in 1215. It has never been formally accepted by the Greek Church and remains an issue of fundamental disagreement.

At first glance this might appear to be yet another example of semantics over substance, but in reality it does reflect a number of differing sensibilities which have been long-standing features within the respective Churches. One such difference is the attitude towards credal formulations, which in the Latin Church have tended to be viewed primarily as doctrinal statements, whereas the Greek Church is inclined to venerate creeds as having almost the same status as Scripture and therefore carrying at least a 'hint' of immutability.

Greek and Latin theologies are also likely to view the procession of the Spirit differently because of the incompatibility of their trinitarian framework, as outlined above. In particular, this applies to the different way in which the person and work of the Spirit is understood in the economy of salvation. It needs to be remembered also that the Latin Church attempted to coerce the Greek Church into accepting change and then simply proceeded unilaterally to ratify the provision, with both of these actions still not forgiven by the Greeks.

Is there a solution here? In the opinion of Francis-Xavier Durrwell, the key to the problem of the procession of the Spirit is to be found in the mystery of the Spirit itself. In his view, it is clear from Scripture that the two terms, the 'Spirit of God' and the 'Power of God', are inextricably linked, such that the

Spirit is God's power at work – or, in trinitarian language, 'in God, the Spirit is the working person'. Furthermore, the Spirit is never presented as the effect of God's action – it is that action.[18]

As examples, God is the Father who begets, the Son is begotten in the world and the Spirit is the all-powerful action in which the work is accomplished. In the Easter event, when the mystery of the Trinity is realised and revealed, it is the Father who arranges the act of resurrection which affects the Son while the Spirit is the power of the resurrection (Romans 8:11). This continuous interrelationship or interdependence highlights the mystery of the *perichoresis* of the Trinity, in which the Spirit can be seen as the movement at the beginning and everywhere.[19]

Against this background, to deny the Son any participation in the procession of the Spirit would not honour the holy *perichoresis* of the Trinity. The Father's 'monarchy' (i.e. unbegottenness) would become a domination, the Son would receive in passivity without responding to the Father, and the Spirit itself would be reduced to being sent after the Son, the last person of the three in whom the movement of the Trinity would run up against a dead end.[20]

In other words, to hold that the Father produces the Son on the one hand and the Spirit on the other does preserve the belief in three persons, but as Durrwell has queried, 'Is it Trinitarian?' In his view, 'if the Spirit were produced in this way, the Father (who is still essentially Father) would not be acting as Father because the Spirit would proceed from him apart from the mystery of the begetting of the Son. The Son would appear neither as Son nor as God, since he would be produced apart from the mystery of the Spirit of which we know that it is the divine begetting, that it is in person all that one can say of the divine nature.'[21]

I am conscious of reaching the point where further comments along these lines could lead us unhelpfully deeper into the realm

[18] Durrwell, *The Spirit of the Father and the Son*, p. 19.
[19] ibid., p. 20.
[20] ibid., p. 59.
[21] ibid., p. 59.

of the abstract. This seems to be the view also of Durrwell, who questions why we should try to fix in a single precise formula what is an inexpressible complexity and suggests that with considered thought a more general formula could be satisfactory, 'even if it were only a tentative approximation'.[22]

It is evident at the present time that there is some distance to go before a meeting of minds on this topic might be possible between the Greek and Latin Churches. As this has been described by Theodore de Regnon, the respective Churches ought to be regarded as two sisters who love and visit each other but have a different way of keeping house and therefore live apart.[23]

A doctrine of the Trinity?

Given the complexity of the subject matter and the animosity that it has generated over the centuries, Colin Gunton, in his book *Father, Son and Holy Spirit*, asks the question, 'What is the point of the doctrine of the Trinity?' He then proceeds with his own answer by providing an outline of what he considers to be the essential message of the doctrine.[24] By way of summary, we might make the following points.

1. If we accept the image of St Irenaeus – that God operates through his two hands, the Son and the Spirit – then this is how God makes himself known; this is his action and presence with us, what he is and what he is always like. In some way, therefore, God must be Father, Son and Spirit to the heart of his being, so the doctrine of the Trinity allows us to identify God who comes among us in this way and enables us to see as much as we need of his nature.

---

[22] ibid., p. 63.
[23] Referred to by LaCugna in *The Trinitarian Mystery of God*, p. 185.
[24] Gunton, *Father, Son and Holy Spirit*, pp. 11–18.

2. The doctrine helps us to avoid slipping into two opposing errors of making God so 'blankly singular' that he loses the richness and plurality of his being and involvement in the world, or of so strengthening the 'threeness' that there could appear to be three Gods. Rather, it is God the Father, God the Son and God the Holy Spirit who together make up all there is of the being of God: what you see is what you get. God is therefore this particular kind of being, not the god of the heathen or of our human projections of what we think god ought to be. He is one God, only in this way to be loved, worshipped and praised in the unutterable richness of his being.

3. The doctrine of the Trinity enables us to see what 'person' means in the context of the divine life and to consider how this might, in turn, help us to understand better what personally being for us is actually about. A key element in the communion which is the Trinity is that in God the three persons are such that they receive from and give to each other a unique particularity. They have a being in relation to each other – the Son is not the Father, the Father cannot be the Father without the Son, and so on.

Father and Son are persons because they enable each other to be truly what the other is; they neither assert themselves at the expense of the other, nor lose themselves in the being of the other. There are not three Gods, because in the divine being a person is one who is so bound up with the being of the other two that together they make up only one God.

Transposed to our level as created beings, we too are able to focus on particularity and relationships. In other words, we have our being not as individuals but because of what we give to and receive from God and one another. We are what God and other people enable us to be or prevent us from becoming. We are the people we are because we are the children of particular parents, the wives or husbands of particular spouses, members of a particular faith community, and so on.

This highlights the old adage, 'No man is an island entire of himself', but in our contemporary society we seem to be losing the sense that we belong with one another. We are inclined not to be concerned with others except as the object of our different needs as they arise from time to time. How much emphasis is placed today on the 'virtue' of self-sufficiency?

And yet accompanying this trend towards self-centred existence, we are increasingly becoming depersonalised, swallowed up into the one mass where individuality is suppressed in the interests of supposed efficiency and economics. For all its apparent pluralism, the world of the market that so dominates our lives is actually geared to making us more homogeneous, to make all of us eat and drink the same 'cool' products, wear the same 'designer' styles, acquire the same 'advanced' technology items, and even take up the offer of plastic surgery to help us look alike.

The Trinity serves to remind us of our particularity, to remind us that it is important to be uniquely what we are ourselves and not a copy of others, but at the same time existing in relationship – to God, to other people and to the world from which we come. Particularity means precisely that: a vast range of ways of being and of being in relationship, all of which are in different ways personal. God's triune personal being stands as a model for ours, an existence in which all accept their need of one another while enabling all to be truly themselves.

4. It is evident that the three persons who make up the being of God are bound together in such a way that only one word in our vocabulary can effectively describe this relationship: 'love'. We are frequently told that God is love and, to my mind, the doctrine of the Trinity

shows something of what that really means and stands as the example for us to try to emulate in our relationships.

In summary, the Trinity is the specifically Christian way of speaking about God. As this is described by Catherine LaCugna:

The heart of Christian life is the encounter with a personal God who makes possible both our union with God and communion with each other. The Spirit of God gathers us together into the body of Christ, incorporating us into a new relationship with each other. Everything is created by God through Christ; all of creation is to be reunited with God (Father) through Christ in the Spirit.[25]

This matches the picture which was presented by St Irenaeus all those centuries ago, of God acting in the world through the Son and Spirit as his two hands. The common denominator is that we are able to identify and come to know God by means of his involvement in our history, in creation, the incarnation of Jesus and the offer of divine life through the power of the Spirit. This is how we are able to understand God's essential and eternal being: 'There is no independent insight into God.' The theology of God is the theology of the Trinity.[26]

The doctrine of the Trinity is a means for us to begin to understand that creation is first of all an act of love, of God enabling things to be themselves externally but in continuing relationship to himself. It highlights for us what it is to be personally, which is not as isolated individuals but as beings who exist in relation to God and to each other. This is a way of living collectively while retaining our own particularity free from any form of coercion.[27]

[25] LaCugna, *The Trinitarian Mystery of God*, p. 155
[26] ibid., p. 154.
[27] Gunton, *Father, Son and Holy Spirit*, p. 14.

It is sometimes suggested that the Trinity is a topic for specialists and unsuitable for general parish preaching, but would God choose to communicate himself in a way that is likely to be wholly unintelligible to the majority? There is no denying the complexity of the subject when viewed from a purely human standpoint, but this did not deter St Patrick, if we believe the story of his explanation using the simple example of a shamrock. Could we not produce similar analogies and present them in image forms suited to this present generation, rather than leaving the doctrine with the 'specialists' where it is likely to remain an abstract concept, aptly described by Karl Rahner as 'locked into splendid isolation with an inherent risk of being found devoid of interest'?[28]

The doctrine of the Trinity is the Christian theology of God. It is our theology and needs to be more coherently explained, more positively proclaimed and more energetically practised. Moreover, for the Spirit – which is the sign of unity within the Trinity – to be a continuing cause of disunity between the Eastern and Western Churches can only be regarded as a scandal.

It is surely time for our respective ecclesiastical leaders to acknowledge that the 'filioque' issue cannot simply be left unresolved. It touches directly on how we understand the person and work of the Holy Spirit and therefore has a bearing on all aspects of Church life. As this has been described by the Russian theologian Vladimir Lossky, 'because of the introduction of the *filioque* clause in the Western Church, the people of God are subjected to the body of Christ, the charism is made subordinate to the institution, inner freedom to imposed authority, prophetism to juridicism, mysticism to scholasticism, the laity to the clergy, the universal priesthood to the ministerial hierarchy and finally the college of bishops to the primacy of the Pope.[29]

Does anything here ring a distant bell?

---

[28] LaCugna, *The Trinitarian Mystery of God,* p. 173.
[29] ibid., p. 184.

Part Two

Our Response To God

5

The Catholic Church

The Catholic Church has been around for almost two thousand years and is able to claim a present 'club membership' equivalent to one in six of the world population. Its history is the history of many nations in terms of the development of their legal, educational, cultural and social frameworks. But what is the Church? What is its purpose and what does membership entail? What do approximately 1.2 billion people think they are about when they wake each morning and how do they measure their performance at the end of each day?

Contemporary wisdom has us believe that the answer to any question can be found through Google.[1] The several search results under the heading 'Catholic Church' indicate that the Church is one of the oldest institutions in the world and is led by the Pope, who as Bishop of Rome is considered by Catholics to be the successor of St Peter. The Pope's office is called the papacy and his ecclesiastical jurisdiction is referred to as the Holy See – a recognised sovereign entity with which international diplomatic relations can be maintained.

The Church's mission is defined as spreading the gospel of Jesus Christ, administering the sacraments and exercising charity. Catholic beliefs are summarised in the Nicene Creed and detailed in the Catechism of the Catholic Church. The beliefs are based on Scripture and Tradition and are collectively referred to as the

---

[1] An internet search engine for a wide variety of data, operated by Google Corporation.

'Deposit of Faith' which continues to be interpreted by the Church's magisterium – its teaching authority which has been divinely bestowed on the Pope and his fellow bishops. Solemn definitions concerning matters of faith and morals are guided by the Holy Spirit and in specific circumstances are deemed to be infallible.

The sacraments are stated to be efficacious signs of grace instituted by Christ and entrusted by Him to the Church to aid the spiritual growth of its members. The Catechism lists seven sacraments, namely, Baptism, Confirmation, the Eucharist, Penance, Annointing the sick, Holy Orders and Matrimony.

As far as it goes, there is nothing here which is contentious as such, but does it really answer the question of what the Church actually is or properly explain our collective vocation? What about the notion of the Church that Vatican II described as a community of believers, 'a chosen race, a royal priesthood, a holy nation, a people for his possession ... who in times past were not a people, but now are the people of God'.[2]

This living, community dimension seems to attract limited emphasis or is missing altogether in many current descriptions of the Church. As explained by Francis-Xavier Durrwell, the Church can all too often be thought of principally in its institutional aspect as an instrument for applying the merits of Christ rather than the great Pascal Sacrament by which the risen Jesus encounters men and women in order to gather them into his body in the community of the Holy Spirit'.[3]

The institution itself is seen to comprise an all-male and ordained executive with assumed responsibility over the general membership which is made up of the laity. In the early Church, the 'laity' (from the Greek word *laos*, meaning 'people') undertook key roles that included preaching, catechetical instruction, presiding at the Eucharist and administering the sacraments, but over time the

---

[2] 'Dogmatic Constitution on the Church'; *Lumen Gentium* no. 9, referring to 1 Peter 2:9–10.
[3] Durrwell, *The Spirit of the Father and the Son*, p. 9.

word became used more as a description of the ordinary people who were the presumed recipients of clerical guidance and control.[4]

This is very much how I recall church life as a schoolboy. It was a highly structured and highly regulated organisation in which nothing was left to chance, where virtually all decisions were taken on our behalf and presented with an assurance of authenticity and an expectation of compliance.

There is no shortage of material from acknowledged experts which chronicles the history of the Church over the centuries, the development of its theology (ecclesiology), the lives of the saints and the achievements of individual Popes and Church Councils. I consider that there is little I can add to this collective scholarship and therefore propose instead to offer a personal overview of the Church based on my experience of 'being Catholic' in a contemporary English environment. This falls into three distinct phases.

Being Catholic – the early phase

> You are Peter and on this rock I will build my Church. And the gates of the underworld can never hold out against it. I will give you the keys of the kingdom of heaven. (Matthew 16:18–19)

This extract from the Gospel of St Matthew had a profound effect on me as a schoolboy in the 1950s. Here was a description of God, in the person of Jesus, announcing his intention to create an organisation which would be the repository for his message on earth for the rest of time. Centuries later, I was part of this same organisation, and as a result of a direct line of succession from St Peter it had come under the stewardship at that time of Pope Pius XII (1939–58).

---

[4] *Modern Catholic Encyclopedia*, p.493.

We were taught that no other organisation had been given such a mandate and no other individual had been entrusted with the same level of responsibility as the Pope – the visible head of the Church on earth, the Vicar of Christ, the spiritual head of all Christians. This mandate came with a divine assurance that the Spirit would teach the Church all things and that she would be preserved from error, kept from losing the essential message of Jesus who would be with her always until the end of time.

More than this, we were informed by the *Penny Catechism* that the Pope had a special and personal assurance of 'infallibility' when as Shepherd and Teacher of all Christians he defined a doctrine concerning faith or morals to be held by the whole Church (#93). What more could one ask to sustain confidence in such an organisation and to remain a dutiful Catholic? By the same token, how unfortunate for so many others in the world who had not yet encountered this 'truth' that was the Catholic Church and, in an English context, how sad that people seemed willing to settle for less by remaining within other ecclesial organisations.

The emphasis in our religious education classes was that only the Catholic Church could trace its origins back to the time of Jesus. Only the Catholic Church could therefore hold the doctrines and traditions of the apostles, because through the unbroken succession of her pastors 'she derives her Orders and Mission from them' (#99). It was only a small step from this to reach the often-expressed official view that there was no salvation outside the Catholic Church. This was certainly a reassuring proposition for a seven-year-old looking from the inside, but what of the others? Why on earth were they not queuing up to join the Church? Why was this evidence of history not seen to be conclusive and compelling?

I remember hearing this exclusivity claim for the Church during a Benediction service at which the Anglican mother of a schoolfriend happened to be present. I remember wondering at the time whether she would be upset to hear the claim (assuming she was listening), or whether we would soon learn that she planned to become a

Catholic (which she did not). The point of mentioning the incident is that it was the first time I recollect hearing an overtly Catholic viewpoint other than in an exclusively Catholic gathering, and given the nature of the statement, it did leave me with a slight feeling of unease.

Many years later, I was in a church in Mallorca for a Sunday evening Mass. The majority of the congregation were women, resplendent in their mantillas and frantically wafting fans to counteract the hot, still evening air. The thought struck me that, purely as a fluke of birth, these particular ladies had been born and brought up in an exclusively Catholic environment, thereby making them eligible for salvation. By contrast, my friend's Anglican mother – whom I remember as one of the kindest and most supportive people I had met outside my family – could not be so certain of her future. Something seemed to be inherently wrong with the method of allocating salvation, or at least with the way it was being presented.

Growing up a Catholic in England in the 1950s could, for the most part, suggest a working-class or lower-middle-class background, an urban environment and close family ties with Ireland. We constituted a fairly close-knit group and we were bought up with an engendered sense of being in some way different and removed from the wider and predominantly Protestant community around us. Catholic families tended to know and socialise with each other, with parish-sponsored events accounting for a majority share of leisure time.

In most parishes, the parish priest had at least one assistant priest (curate) and home visitations were a standard feature of pastoral ministry. In addition to Mass, Benediction and the provision of the sacraments, parishes often ran a variety of lay societies, fraternities and associations. The Church had recently secured government approval (and an element of funding) for Catholic schools and supporting initiatives to raise money for ongoing Catholic school building programmes had almost become an eleventh commandment.

Catholics in the 1950s and early 1960s could be said to constitute an identifiable subgroup within the wider community, which in some instances did give rise to tensions or even hostilities between different faith loyalties. Happily, this was not my experience as we Catholics were presumably not seen as a threat to any established norms. I suspect that we were sometimes thought of as having a number of 'odd' notions or practices, but provided these were kept in-house there was nothing to prevent us from becoming integrated into the social fabric of the neighbourhood. Despite our possible oddity, it is perhaps interesting to compare the number of people electing to join the Church then compared with now.

In my view, the rhythm of Catholic life at this time is brilliantly captured in Eamon Duffy's book *Faith of our Fathers*.[5] This describes Sunday Mass, fortnightly confessions (for some it was weekly), daily rosaries, fish on Fridays, novenas, indulgences, religious icons and processions. Aside from the major feast days and holy days of obligation, there was a discernible programme for the Church's year. May was the month of Mary, October the month of the rosary and November the month for the souls in purgatory. Lent was a challenge for the entire family to endure hardships of one sort or another for six long weeks.

Our Lady featured prominently in our prayer life and the 1950s were an active Marian decade. This began in 1950 with the Dogmatic Pronouncement by Pope Pius XII of the 'Assumption of Our Lady into Heaven', and we were frequently reminded how fortunate we were to have been alive to witness this exercise of papal infallibility. Three years later the Pope declared 1953 a Marian year to be celebrated by the Universal Church, and in 1958 we celebrated the centenary of Mary's appearance to St Bernadette at Lourdes. I well remember also the Rosary Crusade led by the American priest Father Patrick Peyton, which involved large multi-parish rallies that were held at football grounds or

---

[5] Eamon Duffy, *Faith of our Fathers* (Continuum, 2004).

other large public venues and from which came the motto 'The family that prays together stays together'.

Most, if not all, Catholic homes displayed crucifixes and statues and every Catholic I knew had at least one set of rosary beads. We all managed to accumulate numerous medals and holy pictures which were kept in a variety of prayer books and Sunday missals. The focal point of our week was, of course, Sunday Mass, which was an automatic presumption for everyone in the family and around which all activities or other commitments had to be organised.

In our parish we had three Sunday choices. The elderly and the devout tended to go to the 7.30 a.m. Mass, families with children usually chose the 9.30 a.m. Mass, with the rest of us managing (just) to make the 11.00 a.m., which was generally a 'Sung Mass' with incense. There were no evening Masses in those days and to receive Holy Communion it was necessary to have fasted from midnight the day before. For the religiously athletic there was the Rosary Sermon and Benediction on Sunday evenings, and altar boys were often required to make a third visit to the church to serve at Baptisms which for some reason were always held at 3.00 p.m. on Sundays.

Mass was said by the priest in Latin, but the Epistle and Gospel were read out later in English. The priest faced the altar with his back to the congregation and the whole ceremony was highly choreographed down to the detail of individual movements and gestures. For example, having elevated the host during the consecration, the priest was required to keep his index finger and thumb together to avoid any consecrated crumb being accidentally discarded. As an altar boy I remember anxiously concentrating so as not to miss sight of the priest purposely placing his left hand on the altar, which signalled that he had finished his silent reading of the Epistle and it was then my responsibility to move the missal to the other side of the altar so that he could begin reading the Gospel, again in silence.

The laity had no active role. Some of the congregation would follow the order of service using their Sunday missals, others would say the rosary, but many would simply kneel in silent reflection. Being present was the criterion to fulfil one's Sunday obligation, and I remember being told that provided one was physically present from the offertory through to the priest's Communion, this would be sufficient to be able to claim that you had 'heard Mass'. The individual readings and even the reception of Holy Communion almost seemed to be optional extras.

Despite this, there was still for me a sense of something special at each Mass. There was nothing for us to question or discuss regarding the overall content and format of the Mass, as this was how we assumed it had always been and that was all there was to it. Our *Penny Catechism* listed four purposes for the Mass, namely, to give honour and glory to God, to give thanks for all our benefits, to satisfy God for our sins and obtain the grace of repentance, and to obtain all other graces through Jesus (#279). We had been taught that every Mass in every church throughout the world was performed in exactly the same way and I remember being told at one parish mission that there was always a Mass in progress somewhere in the world.

The key features of being Catholic in those days might therefore be summarised as 'certainty', 'conformity' and 'community'. Nothing was formally taught unless its content had been scrutinised and declared 'free from error', which in practice tended to apply to virtually all clerical pronouncements. Formal doctrine was frequently presented as a statement of fact without elaborate explanations and was often expressed in absolute terms to leave no doubt about what was considered right or wrong, true or false, good or bad, sacred or profane.

Conformity together with a strong element of uniformity were both regarded as positive factors at that time, when society in general was in a state of flux in the aftermath of the Second World War. Conformity to teaching and ecclesial practices was also offered as proof of the Church's authenticity, in that the same observances were adopted consistently throughout the world despite the widely diverse nationalities, cultures, social and economic backgrounds amongst the different peoples who comprised the one Catholic Church.

Our regular community witness in attending Mass and participating in the sacraments served as a continuing source of encouragement for us as well as presenting a positive image in the wider community. Catholic families were always seen to be 'scurrying off' to a Mass and the pavements outside the local parish church would throng with people of all age groups at the end of each Sunday service. Many parishes held an annual procession around the immediate neighbourhood and Catholics usually represented the principal customer group at the local fish-and-chip shop on Fridays.

On the negative side, I suppose that a combination of certainty and conformity could give rise to what Monsignor Christopher Lightbound has described as 'clockwork Catholicism' – our being wound up as children like clockwork toys to perform certain ritual observances which we continue to carry out in a purely mechanical fashion through to adult life.[6] In other words, there was an outward observance of the rules and notions of religion without us necessarily being driven by a genuine love of God in our hearts.

This, of course, is for each individual to answer by reference to his or her own unique experience, but an encouraged certainty in belief could also carry a risk of our becoming 'stand-offish' or on occasions intolerant to people of other faiths, even including baptised and practising non-Catholic Christians. The final prayer at Sunday Mass (and one which was actually said in English) was for the conversion of England and for the country to return to being the 'Dowry of Mary'.

Catholic children at non-Catholic schools obtained the right to opt out from school assemblies, which by law in the 1950s had to include some religious content. We were not permitted to say prayers with other religious groups and it was necessary to

---

[6] Christopher Lightbound, *The Church Then and Now* (St Paul's, 2004), p. 29.

secure a dispensation from one's parish priest to enter a non-Catholic church for services such as weddings or funerals.

Weddings were perhaps the most serious point of friction between Catholics and people of other faiths or of none. So-called 'mixed marriages' were discouraged and a formal dispensation was (and remains) necessary under Canon Law before the preparatory process could begin. The form of the wedding ceremony itself was highly dependent on the attitude of the local parish priest. A Nuptial Mass was virtually unknown for a mixed marriage and in some instances the wedding ceremony was not even permitted to take place in the sanctuary. The Catholicity of any children from such a marriage was a non-negotiable precondition which had to be formally agreed by both parties for the event to even be considered.

Despite the strictures which we were called upon to observe and the abruptness or even harshness in the way some of the teachings were presented, I still look back with affection on being Catholic in this period. Catholicism was part and parcel of everyday life, as opposed to just one of a number of separate compartments in one's busy weekly schedule, with constant reminders of our religious heritage in the home, at family gatherings, at our Catholic school and at parish events, all of which seemed to point to a bigger cause in which we were all in some way involved. We were not particularly well educated in the whys and wherefores of many faith propositions and much of what we did was by rote, but we did have a distinct and, for many of us, a lasting sense of Catholic identity.

Being Catholic – the middle period

This was the era of Vatican II, the Ecumenical Council which was held in Rome between 1962 and 1965, bringing together the Church's bishops and their theological advisors from around the world. The decision to hold a council was taken by Pope John

XXIII within months of his election to the Papacy in 1958, and the formal announcement of his intention was made on 25 January 1959, which was the last day in that year's Octave of prayer for Christian unity – a cause that quickly became evident as one of the key drivers of Pope John's pontificate.

The underlying aim for the Council was stated by the Pope as being *aggiornamento*, to bring the Church up to date or, to use his often-reported expression, 'to open the windows and let in fresh air'. Most of us at the time had little knowledge of what an Ecumenical Council entailed and what we might expect from it. The Church was as we had always known it and presumed it had always been, which was aptly described some years later as having 'its peace, its certainties, its clarities, its regimentations and its carefully forged chain of command'.[7] Was this capable of improvement?

The decision to hold a council seemed to come as a surprise to the Church as a whole, and no less to the Curia, the Pope's in-house civil service in Rome. After all, it was less than 100 years since the previous Ecumenical Council (Vatican I, 1869–70), which formally confirmed the doctrine of papal primacy and papal infallibility, prompting some people to question why any further council was thought to be necessary. An infallible Pope with his trusted Curia could surely be relied upon to handle all future contingencies.

However, unbeknown to the majority of us at the time, there had been an ongoing struggle behind the scenes between those within the Church seeking to preserve and maintain control of the *status quo* and those wishing to explore a broader understanding and appreciation of the nature of the Church and its relationship with the world in general. With the benefits of modern scholarship, a number of theologians had reopened studies of the Bible, the liturgy, the teachings and insights of the early Church Fathers and the topic of 'ecumenism' in the sense of unity between different beliefs.

---

[7] Gabriel Daley, 'Faith and Theology', *The Tablet*, April/May 1981.

These several theological groups or movements became referred to collectively as *Nouvelle Theologique* ('new theology'), which was intended as a derogatory title in that they were accused by the Curia of trying to introduce new ideas and concepts into established Church teaching. In reality this was the exact opposite of their purpose, which was to examine and better understand the teachings and practices of the early Church as the source of the 'Great Tradition', namely the process whereby particular truths are handed on from generation to generation. These various movements would eventually find their natural expression at Vatican II.

The Council was formally opened by Pope John XXIII in St Peter's Basilica in Rome on 11 October 1962. In his opening address he outlined four principal themes which were to shape its course, namely, the idea of the Council as the celebration of the faith, ever old, ever new; an optimism in the Spirit to dispel prophets of doom; a clear statement of what this particular Council was for; and a novel approach to errors.[8]

For Pope John, authentic doctrine was to be studied and expressed in the light of modern research methods and the language of modern thought. As he said, the substance of an ancient deposit of faith was one thing, and the way in which it was presented was another. As a departure from the traditional practice of many centuries of formally censuring errors, the Pope stated, 'Today the Spouse of Christ [the Church] prefers to use the medicine of mercy rather than severity. She considers that she meets the needs of the present age by showing the validity of her teaching rather than condemnation.'[9] It was a clear signal that the Pope intended Vatican II to be a pastoral event.

The first session of the Council was held on 12 October and was a foretaste of what was to follow. The initial item on the agenda was for the bishops to approve the nominations of people who had been selected to operate the various Council Commissions

---

[8] Referred to by Tony Castle, *Good Pope John and His Council* (Kevin Mayhew, 2006), p. 43.
[9] ibid., p. 44.

96

together with the theological experts (*periti*) who would assist them. This list of key appointments had been previously and purposely compiled by the Curia, but produced an unexpectedly negative response from the bishops who sought and secured an immediate adjournment to allow them time to consult with each other and decide whom they wished to see appointed to these various positions. Thus the first working session of Vatican II lasted only 30 minutes and in the words of Tony Castle, 'the bishops streamed out into the sunshine having regained control of their Council'.[10]

Vatican II was the twenty-first Ecumenical Council of the Church and the first in its entire history to be concerned with the nature and function of the Church itself. It was also the first Council which was subjected to live coverage by the world's media and in its four working sessions between October 1962 and December 1965 the Council Fathers produced four Constitutions, nine Decrees and three Declarations (see Appendix).

There is a wealth of written material and more recently websites[11] which describe the workings of the Council and provide an analysis of the individual documents and the theological input behind the teaching. Sadly, I suspect that for most people who lived through the Council years, Vatican II is likely to be remembered mainly (if not solely) for introducing changes to the Mass, in particular the use of English in place of Latin. One explanation for this, offered by Oxford Professor Emeritus Maurice Wiles, is that people do not usually feel so deeply over matters of faith and statements of doctrine unless they are considered to bear upon the exercise of their piety. Any change to the Mass would undoubtedly have touched many people's sensitivities and therefore remains their principal memory.[12]

A second explanation why Vatican II seems to have become merely a vague recollection for many people concerns the lack of

---

[10] ibid., p. 44.
[11] See www.vatican2voice.org.
[12] Referred to by LaCugna, *The Trinitarian Mystery of God*, p. 163.

any obvious and coordinated programme at the time which sought to properly describe and explain its purpose and results. References to the Council were made from time to time in homilies and commentaries on individual teachings did appear in the popular Catholic press, but given the standard of religious education of the proverbial 'average Catholic', we received only limited help to understand the background to many of the Council's findings and how these fitted within the overall framework of recognised Church teaching.

With the use of the vernacular came greater lay participation in the prayers of the Mass. It became possible to follow the order of the service with greater ease as priests increasingly presided at Mass facing the congregation and a new Roman Missal (Latin and English) was approved for general use by Pope Paul VI in 1970. By coincidence, this was the four-hundredth anniversary of the approval of an earlier missal by Pope Pius V following the Council of Trent.

As a result of Vatican II, it became permissible to receive Holy Communion in the hand and in a standing rather than a kneeling position, although not all parish priests were happy with this provision and it did occasionally result in some unseemly exchanges during Mass. Holy Communion became available under 'both species' and the period of fasting before reception was reduced to only one hour, opening the way for an evening Mass and eventually leading to the introduction of a vigil Mass on Saturday evening or the eve of a holy day which would fulfil the normal obligation.

In due course, members of the laity were invited to become extraordinary ministers of the Word and the Eucharist with a responsibility for the readings (excluding the Gospel) and the distribution of Holy Communion, both at Mass and to sick parishioners who were housebound. A greeting to one's fellow parishioners was introduced (or, more correctly, reintroduced) in the form of a 'sign of peace' in order to emphasise the communal aspect of every Mass.

The Bible readings became known collectively as the 'Liturgy of the Word' to compliment the 'Liturgy of the Eucharist'. We now had four readings each Sunday, two from the Old Testament and two from the New Testament, and to widen the exposure of the congregation to Scripture the readings were organised to follow a three-year cycle which concentrated in turn on individual evangelists. Despite my previous Catholic school education, I have to admit to coming across a number of Gospel incidents and sayings for the first time as a result of these Council provisions.

The variations in the Mass also produced a ripple effect in other areas without these being immediately apparent. The less frequent use of the rosary heralded a decline in its use altogether and Mass on a Sunday evening took over a slot which had previously been reserved for Benediction. In terms of other Catholic practices, saying 'grace' before and after meals became less frequent, as did a reciting of the 'Angelus' at noon and six o'clock. It was no longer necessary to abstain from meat on Friday, so what had previously been a formal law of the Church carrying the penalty of mortal sin for non-compliance was simply and without explanation discarded to the annals of history.

Looking back, it does seem extraordinary that with such a hitherto distinctive and disciplined character, the Church seems to have been allowed to drift into a new *modus operandi* with little apparent coordination to help manage change. This gave rise to uncertainties and concerns amongst many of the faithful and for the first time in my experience widely differing opinions began to be expressed, and not always with the degree of charity that might have been expected. As with most situations where there is a perceived 'management vacuum', a momentum developed for even more change which only served to further exacerbate the level of discord.

Depending on one's individual viewpoint, Vatican II quickly became the standard or the scapegoat for everything that was happening in the Church. As this was described by the French Dominican Yves Congar (one of the Council *periti*):

There was a simplistic practice of applying the pattern 'before' and 'after' to the Council as though it marked an absolute new beginning, the point of departure for a completely new Church which loses the continuity of tradition. Vatican II was one moment; and neither the first nor the last moment in that tradition – just as Vatican I, the Council of Trent and the Councils of history were neither the first nor the last.[13]

In the period immediately following the Council, I believe it is fair to say that the 'progressive wing' amongst the hierarchy and within the Church generally was in the ascendancy and their approach on occasions almost seemed to match the level of zeal that one tends to associate with the Reformers of the sixteenth century. Many changes were introduced with little proper explanation, which only added to the bewilderment and anxiety of many of the laity (and, one suspects, a number of the clergy) as one previously recognised practice after another was modified or swept away altogether.

A defining event during this era occurred in July 1968, with the publication of the Papal Encyclical *Humanae Vitae*, 'Of Human Life'. This was the official response from Pope Paul VI to the question of whether artificial means of birth control were morally licit. The Pope's answer was 'no', in that every act of sexual intercourse between married couples must remain open to the transmission of human life.

The issue of birth control had been debated during the Council, but the Pope had reserved the matter for his personal consideration. A Commission was formed comprising an international group of clergy and laity, both men and women, to study the theological and medical issues. Needless to say, the subject of contraception

---

[13] Yves Congar, ed. A. Stacpoole, *A Last Look at the Council: Vatican II by Those Who Were There* (Geoffrey Chapman, 1986), p. 351.

was firmly in the sights of the media around the world and frequently led to bursts of press speculation on the likely findings.

I recollect that there was a 'leak' from the Commission to the effect that the majority view of the members was in favour of some modification or change to existing Church teaching. This further served to heighten expectations and when the Pope's decision was formally announced the general reaction was one of surprise and incredulity, producing a response within the Church of disappointment, anxiety and concern and, in some instances, even resentment.

There is no doubting that many husbands and wives continued to follow the Church's teaching, but over the years this would progressively become a minority among married couples. Large numbers of people, in anticipation of the outcome, had already begun to use contraceptives and few of these appeared willing to return to approved Church practices. It is not possible to say what pastoral support was sought or given and I suspect it varied from place to place, but there were certainly examples of priests being suspended for being unwilling to forcibly emphasise authorised rulings in their homilies or in their advice in the confessional.

An official statement emerged later from Rome confirming that *Humanae Vitae* was not an infallible pronouncement, but this was judged to be of doubtful benefit. It did nothing to help people's immediate concerns and could be said to undermine the authority of the Pope by implying that assent might not be mandatory. Moreover, if this was not a matter which called for the exercise of the Pope's 'extraordinary magisterium' (infallible teaching authority), then why was this not made clear when the document was issued?

This was a period of soul-searching and anguish for many in the Church whose long-standing practice of total adherence to official teachings had already begun to be less automatic in the questioning atmosphere of the times. For many couples, *Humanae Vitae* proved to be a catalyst for them to cease further active involvement in the Church and there can be no doubting that the document caused a shift in the attitude of the faithful towards Church authority in general. It should be recorded that Pope Paul did not produce another Encyclical during the remainder of his pontificate, preferring instead to issue advisory letters.

With the benefit of hindsight, I consider that most of us were ill prepared for Vatican II as an event and received limited pastoral support subsequently to help explain and constructively implement its recommendations. In the years following the Council an enthusiasm for reform and change remained undiminished in some quarters, providing fuel to a growing movement for retrenchment in others. The previously discernible Catholic features of certainty, conformity and community became obvious casualties and in this respect it could be said to have been a less than happy and constructive period for the Church.

Being Catholic – the latest phase

For many of us still in the Church who lived through the turmoil of the 1960s and 1970s, I suspect that there has been a tendency to 'tread ecclesial water' ever since. It was only comparatively recently that I resolved to investigate the documents and underlying message of Vatican II and, having made the effort, three things seem to me to be apparent.

1. The *aggiornamento* so earnestly sought by Pope John XIII was long overdue.
2. The comparative lack of detail and guidance on Council teachings during and in the immediate aftermath of Vatican II represents a serious lapse of responsibility by our pastoral leadership.
3. There are signs that an even greater tragedy could be in prospect in the way that many of the teachings of the Council now seem to be becoming marginalised or simply ignored.

The need for Vatican II

I believe an appropriate starting point can be traced back to the Council of Trent, which represented the formal Catholic response to the sixteenth-century Protestant Reformation in Europe. The three sessions of Trent (1543–63) reaffirmed a number of Catholic doctrinal principles (the role of Scripture and tradition, justification, original sin, the effectiveness of the sacraments) as well as introducing a range of Church reforms involving the liturgy and the training of priests. The impact of Trent is evidenced by the fact that the Church's ecclesiology remained largely unchanged for the next 400 years.

This same period coincided with major changes in civil society. The discovery of new continents, the emergence of democratic nation states, industrialisation and urbanisation all contributed to a different order and scale of priorities that were no longer instigated and orchestrated by the Church. The *Christianitas* of medieval Europe – the partnership of Church and state (and always understood in that order!) – no longer carried sway and the loss of the Papal States in Italy to the Nationalists in the mid-nineteenth century even caused some to question whether the Pope would be able to continue to govern the Church.

In the intellectual sphere, the eighteenth century saw the emergence of the Enlightenment, whose proponents, as described by the *Encyclopedia*, introduced the idea of religious toleration but downgraded religious belief, tradition and authority in the intellectual pursuits and emphasised reason as the path to truth and human well-being.[14] Significant advances were also made in the natural sciences to include the theory of evolution of the species.

These were topics which had been thought of as exclusively Catholic territory and in response to what was considered to be society's overtly secular (even anti-Catholic) aims, the Church became progressively introspective and defensive. In 1864, Pope Pius IX issued a *Syllabus of Errors* comprising the wholesale condemnation of a wide range of contemporary theses, which

---

[14] *Modern Catholic Encyclopedia*, p. 283.

supplemented an existing *Index* of books which had been considered dangerous for the faithful (including theologians) and which were banned under threat of excommunication.

There was at least some awareness and concern for the needs of society which prompted an Encyclical from Pope Leo XIII in 1892 titled *Rerum Novarum* ('New Things') in defence of the rights of workers. However, support for papal involvement in this field of activity was by no means unanimous within the Church and subsequent Popes who sought to influence political excesses or attempted to broker peace settlements met with limited success. In the words of Ronald Musto, the modern state was at best indifferent to Christian goals and at worst nakedly hostile to them.[15]

In the field of theology, the standard curriculum at the time of Trent was the teaching of St Thomas Aquinas (1225–74), a leading proponent of Scholasticism – a system of thought and an intellectual approach to religion which was associated with the scholars of the medieval universities. Unfortunately, the way in which some of Aquinas's work was interpreted subsequently did not always accurately reflect his original intentions and in due course this became a further contributory factor in the process of estrangement between the Church and civil society.

Under this general heading, I consider that specific mention needs to be made of the relationship between 'nature' and 'grace' and the way in which this is treated when seeking to describe our human condition. In other words, as a result of our belief of being created in the image and likeness of God, the way in which we view the inbuilt orientation or desire which we claim is always directed beyond the finite towards God.

This 'added dimension' was certainly understood in the early Church, where there was no difficulty or confusion in the blending between the natural and the supernatural components of our human make-up. As this was described by St Irenaeus, 'The glory

---

[15] Ronald G. Musto, *The Catholic Peace Tradition* (Orbis Books, 1986), p. 174.

of God is man alive and the life of man is the vision of God.' Years later, St Augustine would state, 'You have made us for yourself [Lord] and our heart is restless until it rests in you.' This same truth was again expressed by St Thomas Aquinas, that every intellect naturally desires the vision of the divine substance, but later theologians drove a wedge between his use of these two components such that natural desire was only deemed to exist for things with a natural end and a further intervention by God was deemed to be necessary to implant a desire for things supernatural.[16]

This may seem a minor point of difference, but the so-called theory of 'pure nature' which developed out of this changed perspective has produced serious consequences over the ensuing centuries. In the words of Paul McPartlan, the Church traditionally had something to say to everybody because it knew the same natural desire was always seeking its higher fulfilment, but without this Christianity had little to say to those who happily claimed to be able to do without it and/or had not yet received the requisite supernatural call from God. Philosophy and theology moved from being open to each other to being closed realms which could travel their different ways. Philosophy could proceed without any account of religion.[17]

Over time, this gave rise to what the French theologian Henri deLubac (1896–1981) described as a 'separated theology', where all encounters between faith and the world outside are assigned to apologetics, a defensive method of argumentation. In deLubac's view, theology itself became thought of as the science of revealed truths for which an understanding of the faith was a matter of drawing ever more numerous and ever more remote conclusions, but was no longer an understanding of all reality *through the faith*.[18]

This was how attitudes remained up to Vatican II, with formal

---

[16] Referred to by Paul McPartlan, *Sacrament of Salvation* (T. & T. Clark, 1995), p. 49.
[17] ibid., p. 51.
[18] Referred to by Joseph Komonchak, *Theology and Culture at Mid-Century: The Example of Henri deLubac* (Theological Studies 51, 1990), p. 582.

Church policy being described by the historian and theologian Joseph Komonchak as a 'domesticated theology', by which he meant that it came under the closest supervision and tightest control that theologians had ever experienced and was a discipline which was taken seriously only, or at least chiefly, within the Catholic subculture.[19] A different approach was necessary.

The Vatican II Years

Vatican II was the twenty-first Ecumenical Council in the history of the Church and comprised by far the largest and most representative gathering of bishops. For example, around 200 European bishops had attended the sixteenth-century Council of Trent, which increased to approximately 800 and still mainly European bishops at Vatican I. At the solemn opening ceremony of Vatican II there were 2,450 bishops in attendance, together with 45 observers from other Christian Churches. Reporting on the procession of bishops at the opening ceremony in St Peter's Basilica in October 1962, the correspondent for *Time* magazine reported, 'My first impression was of the immense universality of the Church. I saw black faces, yellow faces, brown faces; from a distance it was like a waterfall of every colour of the rainbow. These were the representatives from around the world of Church.'[20]

Vatican II could be said to have signalled the coming of age of the Church as a truly global entity and the scale of its concern and perceived mission is evident from the number of documents which were debated and agreed. For present purposes I propose to focus briefly on just three of the approved documents. (NB: The conventional practice with official documents involves referring to them by using their opening words in Latin.)

---

[19] ibid., p. 579.
[20] Referred to by Castle, *Good Pope John and His Council*, p. 43.

'Constitution on the Sacred Liturgy': *Sacrosanctum Concilium (SC)*

It is not by coincidence that this was the first document to be approved at Vatican II, as it reflects the importance which the bishops attributed to the liturgy (public worship) in the life of the Church. 'For the liturgy, through which the work of our redemption takes place, especially in the divine sacrifice of the Eucharist, is supremely effective in enabling the faithful to express in their lives and portray to others the mystery of Christ and the real nature of the true church' (*SC #2*).

'The liturgy then is rightly seen as an exercise of the priestly office of Jesus Christ ... From this it follows that every liturgical celebration, because it is an action of Christ the priest and of his body which is the Church, is a pre-eminently sacred action. No other action of the church equals its effectiveness by the same title nor to the same degree' (*SC #7*). The liturgy is rightly called '... the summit towards which the activity of the Church is directed; it is also the source from which all its power flows' (*SC #10*).

This is a far cry from Mass being viewed simply as a weekly ceremony of conformity or obligation, and the 'pastors of souls' were urged to realise that their responsibility went beyond just observing the laws governing liturgical celebrations and they were required to ensure that the faithful took part fully aware of what they were doing, actively engaged in the rite and enriched by it (*SC #11*). They were also charged with the task of promoting a warm and lively appreciation of sacred Scripture (*SC #24*).

Acknowledging the cultural diversity which exists within the Church, *Sacrosanctum Concilium* was anxious not to impose a rigid liturgical uniformity, but rather to cultivate and foster the qualities and talents of various races in matters not affecting the underlying faith and well-being of the entire community (*SC #37*). Subject to prior approval by the Apostolic See, bishops in individual territories were given leave to admit adaptations to the liturgy which they considered useful or necessary, having regard to prevailing cultural and educational conditions (*SC #40*).

Contrary to popular belief, it should be noted that the Council Fathers proposed that Latin should be preserved in all rites and called for care to be taken to ensure that the faithful were able to say or sing together in Latin those parts of the Ordinary of the Mass which pertain to them (*SC #54*). However, the use of an approved translation into the vernacular could be adopted if and when it was considered to be of advantage to the faithful (*SC #36*).

'Dogmatic Constitution on the Church': *Lumen Gentium (LG)*

In response to the call by Pope John XXIII for the Church to re-evaluate its purpose and function, *Lumen Gentium* is the cornerstone document of Vatican II. The title of its opening chapter is 'The Mystery of the Church', which declares that the Church, in Christ, is a sacrament – a sign and instrument of communion with God and of the unity of the entire human race (*LG #1*). By communicating his Spirit, Christ mystically constitutes as his body his brothers and sisters from every nation (*LG #7*).

We begin then to understand the Church as something that is alive within us, not simply an organisation but rather an organism of the Holy Spirit, constantly sustained here on earth as a community of faith, hope and charity. We are the body of Christ. He is the head, we are the members and through this visible society and spiritual community, Christ communicates truth and grace to everyone (*LG #8*).

This is the unique Church of Christ which, in our Sunday Credo, we profess to be 'one, holy, catholic and apostolic'. However, in a marked departure from earlier claims of exclusivity, *Lumen Gentium* states, 'This Church, constituted and organised as a society in the present world subsists in [as opposed to 'is'] the Catholic Church, which is governed by the successor of Peter and by the bishops in communion with him' (*LG #8*). In other words, there is an acknowledgement that many elements of sanctification and truth are found outside the Church's visible confines.

This opening-out process is taken a step further by the second chapter, which is entitled 'The People of God', a term that represents a broad constituency within which to consider the relatedness of the Roman Catholic Church to other Christians' affiliations as well as to non-Christians (*LG* #15, 16). There is also an historical dimension to the concept of the people of God that can be found in the Old Testament. Tracing the ongoing unity of God's involvement with a particular people and looking to the future, this gives shape to the idea of a pilgrim Church, always on the move, continually in need of renewal, not yet having reached its end goal (*LG* #48).

Lumen Gentium reaffirmed that in the early Church, the centrality and prominence of the Eucharist was fundamental to its identity and purpose. As Paul McPartlan reminds us, even before a formal creed had been finalised, Christians gathered in local communities week in and week out to 'celebrate' their faith.[21] The community which is the Church is therefore, at its heart, a 'eucharistic community'. In the memorable expression of Henri deLubac, one of the principal theological experts at Vatican II, 'The Eucharist makes the Church.'[22]

In every celebration of the Eucharist, Christ gives himself complete and undivided, hence *Lumen Gentium* declares that 'the Church of Christ is really present in all legitimately organised local groups of the faithful which united with their pastors are also called churches in the New Testament' (*LG* #26). The clear import of this is that each (legitimately organised) local community is itself a complete manifestation of the Church, as 'it is in and from these that the one true unique Catholic Church exists' (*LG* #23). In other words, the universal Church is represented by the local Churches and it is within them that it becomes a tangible

---

[21] McPartlan, *Sacrament of Salvation*, p. 34.
[22] ibid., p. 30.

reality – a 'communion of communions' – in stark contrast to what I had previously understood (or been taught?), namely, that my parish was merely a branch or a tiny offshoot of the major international entity which Jesus had gifted to St Peter and his successors in perpetuity.

The interface between each local church and the universal Church is shown to reside in the bishops, who by divine institution are stated to have taken the place of the apostles as pastors of the Church with collective responsibility for its well-being (*LG* #20). As such, *Lumen Gentium* reaffirmed the earlier understanding of episcopal consecration as conferring the 'fullness of the sacrament of Orders ... the summit of the sacred ministry which is placed within a framework of Episcopal Collegiality' (*LG* #21, 22).

The concept of collegiality amongst the bishops is traceable back to the original Twelve called by Jesus (Mark 3:13–14), who would combine with each other to form a community with Peter as their lead spokesman. In like fashion, *Lumen Gentium* provides that the Roman Pontiff as Peter's successor and the bishops as successors of the apostles are joined together and constitute a collegiate community and structure. Installed throughout the world, they live in communion with one another and with the Roman Pontiff in a bond of unity, charity and peace (*LG* #22).

Lumen Gentium rightly includes a section devoted to Our Lady, who is acknowledged and honoured as truly the Mother of God and the Redeemer (LG #53). She is a 'type' of the Church in the order of faith, charity and perfect union with Jesus (LG #63), as well as being mother to us in the order of grace (LG #61).

To summarise *Lumen Gentium*, we are being called to visualise a pilgrim Church which is alive in the hearts of the faithful, and whenever and wherever we assemble to celebrate the Eucharist we become the fullness of the Church as a result of our communion with other Churches and with the Roman Pontiff. Seen in this light, our unity of faith is able to support a broad diversity in respect of culture, status and history, reflecting a universal call to holiness in accordance with God's will (Ephesians 1:4).

'Pastoral Constitution on the Church in the Modern World':
Gaudium et Spes (GS)

This document was created in response to the wish of Pope John XIII for Vatican II to be a pastoral Council. It was also the only document which had not been outlined and circulated in draft form prior to the Council opening, because the decision to produce what eventually became *Gaudium et Spes* was not actually taken until the end of the first session in December 1962. Credit for its introduction is generally accorded to the Belgian Cardinal Leon-Joseph Suenens.

I believe the opening paragraph of *Gaudium et Spes* merits being quoted in full.

> The joys and hopes, the grief and anguish of the people of our time and especially those who are poor or afflicted, are the joys and hopes, the grief and anguish of the followers of Christ as well. Nothing that is genuinely human fails to find an echo in their hearts. For theirs is a community of people united in Christ and guided by the Holy Spirit in pilgrimage towards the Father's Kingdom, bearers of a message of salvation for all of humanity. That is why they cherish a feeling of deep solidarity with the human race and its history. (*GS* #1)

By this statement, the Church formally signalled its intention to return to the world and re-engage with society as a whole, with a policy of remaining attuned to 'the signs of the times' (*GS* #2). As an added measure of the change in attitude which had occurred over the 100 years since Pius IX's *Syllabus of Errors*, there came the acknowledgement that the relationship between the Church and the world should be a two-way exercise of mutual interaction. Even more startlingly, there was also an admission that the Church was willing to accept how richly she has profited by the history and development of humanity (*GS* #44).

Gaudium et Spes is the longest document produced by the Council and is arranged in two parts. Part One develops Church teaching about humanity and the world in which we live by considering issues such as the dignity of the human person, the community of mankind, human activity and the role of the Church. Part Two looks at several aspects of modern living and in particular the problems of the time in terms of marriage and the family, sexual relationships, socio-economics, ownership, war and peace.

To take some specific examples, *Gaudium et Spes* admits to the autonomy of humanity and of organisations and science in the discovery, utilisation and ordering of the laws and values of matter and society, provided these do not override moral laws or conflict with them (*GS* #36). The Church recognises the dignity of each person to act out of conscience and free choice, in contrast to simply being led by blind impulses or external constraints (*GS* #17). All Christians are warned of the dichotomy between the faith they profess and their day-to-day conduct, and are urged to avoid a 'pernicious opposition' between their professional and social activities on the one hand and their religious life on the other (*GS* #43).

In terms of urgent problems, the practice of 'responsible parenthood' enters the Catholic vocabulary, whereby married couples arrive in judgement before God through the exercise of their conscience, albeit this conscience should reflect the teaching authority of the Church as the interpreter of the Law of God (*GS* #50). In the sphere of war and peace, *Gaudium et Spes* contains the strongest condemnation (in fact the only outright condemnation to be found in any of the Council documents) expressed against the total destruction of cities or other extensively populated areas, i.e. the use of nuclear weapons, which is defined as 'a crime against God' (*GS* #81).

And so, three years and two months after its opening ceremony, Vatican II was formally closed by Pope Paul VI, on 8 December 1965, the feast of the Immaculate Conception of Mary, the Mother of the Church. In his closing decree the Pope declared that all

Catholics were bound by the Council's decisions and all actions undertaken knowingly or through ignorance against such teachings were invalid.[23]

The 16 approved documents of Vatican II can be seen to represent a promising start towards achieving the *aggiornamento* so earnestly sought by Pope John XXIII. However, a few years later the theologian Yves Congar expressed concern at the danger for the Church in not seeking anything more and simply exploiting the inexhaustible warehouse of Vatican II. In his judgement this would result in a post-Vatican II era opening up in the same way as a post-Tridentine (Council of Trent) era had existed. It would, he said, be a betrayal of the *aggiornamento* if we thought it could be fixed once and for all in the text of Vatican II.[24] This was a highly prophetic observation, given the way events seem to be transpiring.

The post-Vatican II Church

I would like to recount three additional observations. The first is from Cardinal John Henry Newman following Vatican I, when he wrote that it was rare for a Council not to be followed by great confusion. His opinion was based on a detailed study of Church Councils right back to Nicea in 325, which had been 'followed by 60 years of contentions, punctuated by synods, excommunications, exiles, interventions and Imperial acts of violence'.[25] Happily we have been spared the worst of such excesses in the wake of Vatican II, but there has certainly been a period of confusion which has sometimes been punctuated by acrimonious exchanges between those with differing viewpoints.

The second observation comes from the then Father Joseph Ratzinger, who shortly after Vatican II stated:

---

[23] Castle, *Good Pope John and His Council*, p. 121.
[24] Michael Winter, 'On Yves Congar', *Clergy Review 55* (1970), p. 287.
[25] Referred to by Y. Congar, *A Last Look at the Council: Vatican II by Those Who Were There*, p. 349.

Whilst the Council formulated its pronouncements with the fullness of the power that resides in it, its historical significance will be determined by the process of classification and elimination that takes place subsequently in the life of the Church. In this way, the whole Church participates in the Council; it does not come to an end in the assembly of bishops.[26]

Father Ratzinger was referring here to the process known as 'the reception' of a Council, the action of understanding, interpretation and application whereby the principles behind the basic text enter or are assimilated into the conscious practice of the Church. As his statement makes clear, the process involves the whole of the faithful, the *sensus fidei* of a global Church that incorporates the different perspectives of race, culture, geography and local history.

The third observation belongs to the then Abbot Christopher Butler who, at the close of Vatican II, predicted that it would take at least 30 or 40 years for the message of the Council to be fully implemented. A few years later he increased his time frame to 130 years on the grounds that he saw little evidence of a genuine desire, either in Rome or amongst his fellow bishops, fully to promote the teachings of Vatican II.[27]

More than 40 years have now passed since the end of Vatican II and with the ease of access to information and ever-improving means of communication this seems a more than reasonable period over which to expect the principal teachings of the Council to have been transmitted and a good degree of assimilation and implementation already achieved. Sadly, this is not my experience and at best I would describe the flow of information as 'patchy'.

For my generation, I suspect that Vatican II may have become a distant memory, with the principal recollection being the changes it brought about to the Mass. Many younger Catholics appear to

---

[26] Referred to by Ormond Rush, *Still Interpreting Vatican II* (Paulist Press, 2004), p. 53.
[27] Castle, *Good Pope John and His Council*, p. 8.

have little awareness that there was a Council, let alone what teachings were approved. As a result, I believe the majority of the faithful have a limited grasp of the Church as a sacrament, of their vocation and role as the people of God, and of the theology of the local church and the universal Church and its unity and governance by means of episcopal collegiality.

Even with the Mass, where we are taught that 'our sanctification in Christ and glorification of God is achieved with maximum effectiveness' (*SC* #10), it is possible to encounter a wide variety of views concerning its history, form and content. And this is despite the call for the faithful to be made aware of what they are doing and why (*SC* #11). We seem to spend a lot of time arguing about whether the Mass should be in Latin or English and debating individual rubrics, as if these factors constituted the essence of the ceremony.

There is undoubtedly greater lay participation within the Church today, but this could be said to be more of a practical expediency as a result of fewer priests, rather than the result of a particular theological imperative. In my view we are witnessing a return to the same 'pyramid' form of authoritative structure which was a feature of the pre-Conciliar Church. At the apex is the Pope and immediately beneath him is his Curia. The next level down comprises the bishops and under them are their priests. The remainder, at the base of the pyramid, are the laity.

The general presumption is that the Holy Spirit communicates with the Church principally via the apex and directives are then allowed to filter down to lower levels as considered necessary or appropriate. This appears a long way removed from the concept of pastoral leadership envisaged by Vatican II and in my view it is precisely this type of proscriptive, centralised and authoritative model that the Council sought to eliminate with its emphasis on the Church as the people of God and authority understood as service in the building up of God's kingdom on earth.

There seems to be a mindset in some quarters that wishes to see the Church return to the same outlook, approach and structure as before Vatican II. If this is the case, it could arguably be in direct conflict with the express directive which was issued by Pope Paul VI at the close of the Council, binding all Catholics to adhere to its teachings. Moreover, it is surely implicit in this papal directive that the teachings themselves should be communicated as widely as possible within the Church, but in my experience such an exercise has not formed part of any officially devised and sustained programme and this might itself be interpreted as a deviation from papal intent.

Aside from the issue of conformity, I consider that we need to spare a thought also for the post-Vatican II generations of Catholics. They could increasingly find themselves in an organisation that seems determined to return to the past, with its own particular set of ground rules and practices that appear to bear little relationship to the way of life they now know and understand. Can they really be expected to remain actively committed participants?

To summarise my experience of being Catholic, I still retain fond memories of the pre-Conciliar Church with its unquestioning way of life that was defined and sustained by a distinctive range of established devotional practices. Vatican II ushered in an era of change, but with no real explanation of why and little effective support to help with the transition. For a number of the faithful at the time there was a sense of betrayal of their traditional Catholic piety.

Over the intervening years, there seems to have been an intentionally selective approach to the Council rather than an ongoing and comprehensive examination of its findings. As a result, I consider that the majority of today's faithful continue to be unaware of many of the individual teachings and their intended purpose and I regard this as a betrayal of the Spirit-led insights of the Council Fathers and their aspirations for the Church in the modern world.

Vatican II needs to be treated as a whole and understood as a solemn articulation of Catholic tradition, not simply an optional source of reference. My hope for the future is that our pastoral leadership will recognise this and fulfil their responsibilities in the manner proposed by the Council. I hope that they will continue to focus on the 'signs of the times' and on the unfinished business which was referred to by Pope Paul VI, in order to find pastoral solutions which are responsive to the underlying needs of our twenty-first-century Church. In the words of the Pope, *aggiornamento* should mean for us 'an enlightened insight into the Council's spirit and a faithful application of the norms it has set forth in such a felicitous and holy manner'.[28]

---

[28] Rush, *Still Interpreting Vatican II*, p. ix.

6

Authority and Conscience

The dictionary defines authority as 'the power or right to control, judge or prohibit the actions of others'.[1] So is this description of authority equally appropriate in the Church? And if so, where does it reside and in what manner should it be exercised?

A recourse to Scripture does highlight a somewhat different interpretation of authority. As examples, there is the incident when James and John were vying for the highest places in the kingdom, which prompted Jesus to say:

> You know that among the pagans their so-called rulers lord it over them and their great men make their authority felt. This is not to happen among you. No; anyone who wants to become great among you must be your servant, and anyone who wants to be first among you must be slave to all. For the Son of man himself did not come to be served but to serve and to give his life as a ransom for many. (Mark 10:42–45)

In a further incident, Jesus berated the Pharisees for the way they paraded and used their authority and then cautioned his disciples:

> You, however, must not allow yourselves to be called Rabbi, since you have only one Master and you are all brothers.

---

[1] *Collins Dictionary and Thesaurus* (Collins, 1987).

You must call no one on earth your father since you have only one Father and he is in heaven. Nor must you allow yourselves to be called teachers for you have only one Teacher, the Christ. (Matthew 23:8–10)

In my view, these texts serve to illustrate two fundamental characteristics of authority when considered in a Church context. The first is that authority essentially belongs to God, or, more correctly, to the 'Triune God' of Father, Son and Spirit, and titles such as 'lord', 'ruler', 'master' and 'teacher' are due only to Jesus, not his disciples. Second, Jesus is proposing that the basis of power or authority for his followers is that of service with a shared responsibility to serve the coming reign of God in the hearts of all people. As Geoffrey Robinson put it, if some were to be given authority within the community this was solely so they could serve the others and all could serve the reign of God, for which the actions of Jesus would always constitute the rule.[2]

In his book *Ministry and Authority in the Catholic Church*, Edmund Hill examines the distribution of authority within the Church under four principal headings.[3] The first concerns the authority which is due to God and to Christ, which for present purposes we can take as a given. The second looks at authority bestowed by Christ on the Church and all its members, for which several references are traceable within Scripture: for example, 'but to all who receive him, who believed in his name, he gave the power to become children of God' (John 1:12). Quoting from St Paul, 'because you are sons, God has sent the Spirit of his Son into our hearts crying "Abba, Father" so through God you are no longer a slave but a son and if a son then an heir' (Galatians 4:4–7). And there is the offer made to the whole of the faithful, as a 'chosen race' to share in the priesthood and kingship of Christ – both of which are authority roles (1 Peter 2:5, 9).

---

[2] Robinson, *Confronting Power and Sex in the Catholic Church*, p. 82.
[3] Edmund Hill, *Ministry and Authority in the Catholic Church* (Geoffrey Chapman, 1988), pp. 18–21.

The third 'category' of authority is that which was bestowed upon the apostles as part of their commissioning by Jesus: 'and he called to him his twelve disciples and gave them authority [*potestas*, a legal or juridical word in Latin for 'power'] over unclean spirits to cast them out and to heal every disease and every infirmity' (Matthew 10:1). Their instruction was to proclaim that the kingdom was close at hand with the promise that 'he who welcomes you, welcomes me' (Matthew 10:40), which can be taken to mean the acceptance of their teaching, and therefore a kind of authority among and over those who received them.

Finally, there is a specific authority bestowed on St Peter by virtue of his appointment by Jesus as the 'rock' upon which the Church would be built (Matthew 16:18–20). An intention to preserve a specific 'Petrine office' becomes evident from the second letter of St Peter, in which he states that he has a duty to continuously recall the truths of Jesus as long as he is alive, with the promise that he will take great care after his 'departure' for the faithful to have the means to recall things to memory (2 Peter 1:12–15). By virtue of an unbroken line of succession, Catholic teaching holds that the authority which resides in the Petrine office is the prerogative of each successive Pope.

It seems apparent from the above that the primary participation in the authority of Christ lies with the whole body of the faithful, derived through faith as a result of a common baptism and exercised in service to the world. The authority of the bishops and the specific authority of the Pope are therefore meant to be at the service of the Church and all its members for the same purpose.

The precise manner in which these different categories of authority were intended to operate was not specified by Jesus, but the New Testament does identify a number of pointers. For example, the apostles met in Jerusalem to resolve a dispute with the church in Antioch over what conditions, if any, should be imposed on non-Jews wishing to become Christians (Acts 15:1–12). The decision which was announced by St Peter was not his proprietary judgement as leader of the group, but the consensus view of the apostles following debate, and it is a matter of record that this involved a change of heart by St Peter which he admitted as a result of the merits of a counter-argument presented by St Paul.

In terms of the 'apostolic succession', it is interesting to note the wide participation which took place to find a replacement for Judas. We read of candidates' names being put forward for discussion and evaluation, with the eventual selection being achieved by means of casting lots rather than being a summary appointment by St Peter or the original group of apostles (Acts 1:21–26).

In a separate incident, and despite being the acknowledged leader of the disciples, St Peter was called upon by 'the brothers' to justify his conduct in visiting the home of the centurion Cornelius. This had been for the purpose of explaining the faith, but visiting and eating with an uncircumcised person was expressly forbidden for Jews. In Jesus' name, St Peter was able to convince them that his actions had been a true expression of God's will (Acts 11:1–18).

The pattern which can be seen from these examples is that the bestowal of authority did not automatically convey some magical or oracular power on any individual. Reaching conclusions on matters of clarification called for the active collaboration and contribution of others, with eventual decisions and actions still remaining open to scrutiny and accountability.

In the early years of the Church there was a variety of charisms and considerable diversity in the way the local Christian communities were structured and run. Over time, this began to give way to a more uniform pattern of operation and, in particular, a distinction started to emerge between what had been the interchangeable titles of *presbyteroi* ('elders') and *episkopoi* ('supervisors'), or what we now refer to as bishops, whereby the latter assumed a presidency over each local church. In this regard, a bishop can therefore be seen to have come into existence as an 'elevated' presbyter rather than as a localised apostle, prompting the suggestion that the claim of bishops to be successors of the apostles might more correctly be expressed as successors (or heirs) to the 'authority' of the apostles rather than their specific apostolic function.[4]

Papal authority

The most noticeable change in the structure and composition of authority in the Latin (Roman Catholic) Church was the development of papal authority, which progressively eclipsed the authority of the other bishops and extended to claims of absolute and universal sovereignty over all authorities, both civil and ecclesial. This produced frequent wrangles and even wars with secular rulers and was a divisive issue within the Church between the supporters of papal hegemony and advocates of 'conciliarism', who sought to restrain papal ascendancy in governance by means of Church Councils.

Ironically, the pinnacle of papal aspirations for autonomy was attained as a result of a Council, namely the First Vatican Council (1869–70), which formally proclaimed the doctrine of papal primacy and papal infallibility. The principle of a primacy being due to the Pope as successor to St Peter and Bishop of Rome was not new or in itself an issue amongst Catholics, Orthodox and even some Protestant Churches. The problem arose with the Council's definition that the Pope had:

> full and supreme power of jurisdiction over the whole church, not only in matters of faith and morals but also in those which concern the discipline and government of the church dispersed throughout the whole world ... an absolute fullness of this supreme power ... ordinary and immediate both over all and each of the churches and over all and each of the pastors and faithful.[5]

---

[4] ibid., p. 34, quoting the views of Bishop Lightfoot (*Dissertation on the Christian Ministry*, 1868) and Jean Danielou and Henri Marrou (*The Christian Centuries*, 1964).
[5] Quoted by Tanner, *The Councils of the Church: A Short History*, p. 90.

Not surprisingly, the scale of these provisions alienated other Churches and their implications were a matter of concern for a number of Catholics. As observed by Geoffrey Robinson, the Pope became separated from the body of bishops and rather than serving them, they were to serve him. The notion of the Pope as the principle of unity became a notion of the Pope as the principle of direction. The entire universal Church could become treated as 'the Pope's diocese' and the original idea of the diocese of Rome possessing a primacy because it was the place of St Peter's witness vanished in favour of the idea of a Pope possessing a personal primacy because of the words of Jesus in the Gospel of St Matthew.[6]

By way of background, the actual Council document, 'The Constitution on the Church of Christ' (*Pastor Aeternus*), was intended to be a full decree on the Church, but due to external political and military pressure the Council was forced to adjourn early and so the definition of papal primacy emerged in isolation rather than being just one component within a broader ecclesial framework. Moreover, the original draft (or schema) was concerned with the primacy of the Bishop of Rome, but during the course of the debate this became extended to include an infallible teaching authority.

Given the significance of this formal pronouncement, it is worth quoting the full agreed definition of papal infallibility.

> Therefore, faithfully adhering to the tradition received from the beginning of the Christian faith, to the glory of God our Saviour, for the exaltation of the catholic religion and for the salvation of the Christian people with the approval of the sacred council, we teach and define as a divinely revealed dogma that when the Roman Pontiff speaks *ex cathedra*, that is, when, in the exercise of his office as shepherd and teacher of all Christians in virtue of his supreme apostolic

---

[6] Robinson, *Confronting Power and Sex in the Catholic Church*, p. 117.

authority, he defines a doctrine concerning faith or morals to be held by the whole Church, he possesses by the divine assistance promised to him in blessed Peter, that infallibility which the divine Redeemer willed his Church to enjoy in defining doctrine concerning faith and morals. Therefore, such definitions of the Roman Pontiff are of themselves and not by the consent of the church, irreformable.[7]

There are several points within this definition which need to be properly noted. The Pope has to be speaking in solemn form, *ex cathedra* (symbolically his chair of office), and his infallibility must be understood as being part and parcel of the infallibility enjoyed by the whole Church, not something different, outside or in addition to it. The Pope here is the representative of the Church, not of God, and as the text makes clear, he possesses 'that infallibility which the divine Redeemer willed his Church to enjoy'.[8]

In addition, infallibility is only engaged where there is a question of defining doctrine, and to 'define' is a precise term in this context. It does not cover teaching in general, preaching or theological expositions. It is simply and solely the making of a formal – and limiting – judgement in order to clarify the understanding of an existing facet within the Church's deposit of faith.[9]

Even with this explanation it is easy to see how the doctrine identifies the Church with the Papacy, so that expressions such as 'the Church says' or 'the Church teaches' when used in sermons, pastorals and catecheses are often heard (and uttered) as meaning 'the Pope says' or 'the Pope teaches'. This is not to question the office of Pope, but rather the tendency to presume that every statement which emanates from Rome represents a definitive and

---

[7] Quoted by Tanner, *The Councils of the Church: A Short History*, pp. 91–2.
[8] ibid., p. 92.
[9] Hill, *Ministry and Authority in the Catholic Church*, p. 100.

irreformable teaching – what many within the Church describe as 'creeping infallibility'.[10]

Enter the word 'magisterium', which appears of late to be an increasingly used appendage to support official statements – a sort of British Standard or ISO quality accreditation that is intended to boost their importance. The practical effect is that statements which are made under this 'umbrella' can, if repeated regularly, begin to become thought of as almost carrying a stamp of divine origin – what might perhaps be termed 'gradual infallibility'.[11]

The word 'magisterium' (from the Latin *magister*, meaning 'master') needs to be considered not only in the sense of 'teaching' but, in our current context, in the sense of possessing authority or mastery in a particular field.[12] Mindful of Jesus' caution to his disciples only to consider him as teacher (Mathew 23:10), St Augustine repudiated any magisterium for himself while accepting, 'with fear and trepidation', his responsibility as a bishop to teach. Contrast the 1914 Encyclical from Pope Benedict XV on the topic of freedom for theological discussion, in which he stated, 'All know to whom the *magisterium Ecclesia* has been given by God; to this one therefore belongs the complete right to speak as he thinks fit, when he will; the duty of the rest is religiously to comply with the speaker and to be hearer of what is said.'[13]

There are several situations which follow as a result of the way authority is currently practised within the Church. First, our existing hierarchical structure is presented or at least implied as being an exact model of the divine blueprint which was intended for the Church. As if Jesus had fully expected the successor of St Peter to be head of a sovereign state, to run the Church with his own selected Curia, to appoint and manage every brother bishop and take sole responsibility as 'supreme legislator' in matters of administration and discipline (i.e. Canon Law).

---

[10] Robinson, *Confronting Power and Sex in the Catholic Church*, p. 121.
[11] ibid., p. 122.
[12] *Modern Catholic Encyclopedia*, p. 536.
[13] Referred to by Hill, *Ministry and Authority in the Catholic Church*, p. 78.

Second, there is the manner in which official Church teaching is often imparted and sometimes imposed. An example highlighted by Geoffrey Robinson is the 1994 *Catechism*, which he describes as a useful guide to the teachings of the Church, but without proper explanation it can carry the risk of reducing faith to an intellectual assent to a series of propositions rather than it being a response in love from one person to another. Moreover, the *Catechism* is a compilation of infallible statements, definitive but not infallible statements and statements that one presumes are not definitive, with little guidance on which category each might belong to, leading to the tendency for every statement to be upgraded and treated as the yardstick of all authority.[14]

The exercise of authority and conscience

Discussions about authority and conscience have a long history. As described by Avery Dulles, the members of all social groups form their personal moral norms with some dependence on the group and its leaders, and on the basis of these convictions they determine whether to follow the community's authority in given circumstances. To the extent that individuals have been successfully socialised into a community, their free judgement about right and wrong will tend to coincide with the rules and expectations of that community.[15]

Nevertheless, tensions and indeed conflict can occur whenever authority asserts itself and is thought to impose an obligation to assent or obey. An example cited by Dulles is a public authority with a tradition of civil liberties which will recognise the normative value of an individual conscience but must still set limits to what people wish to claim in the name of conscience so as not to trample on the rights of others or jeopardise the common good.

---

[14] Robinson, *Confronting Power and Sex in the Catholic Church*, p. 121.
[15] Avery Dulles, 'Authority and Conscience', from *Readings in Moral Theology*, No. 6 (Paulist Press, 1988), p. 98.

Considered in the context of the Church, authority and conscience involve a significant added dimension. Our belief is that the Church has been established by the action of God in Jesus and is a society of faith and witness which exists only to the extent that it continues to adhere to a specific vision of the world centred on Jesus Christ. Unlike a secular organisation, the Church has a deposit of faith that must be maintained intact and transmitted to new members. It cannot therefore accommodate the same kind of ideological pluralism that may be acceptable in a secular state. Moreover, the members of the Church, including the highest office holders, act as trustees and are not free to change in a substantive way the beliefs, structures, purposes and forms of worship in the Church.[16]

The Catholic tradition has been to treat the hierarchy as part of the promise which Jesus gave to the apostles, that 'whoever hears you hears me' (Luke 10:11), and again, 'as the Father sends me, so I send you' (John 20:20), and this continues to colour the attitude of today's Catholics towards ecclesiastical authority. A particular strand of this which developed over recent centuries is the view that only a strong Papacy is able to protect the Church against oppressive civil laws and heterodox organisations, out of which grew a movement known as Ultramontanism – meaning 'beyond the mountains' and referring to the Alps, beyond which is Rome.

As described by the Augustinian theologian, Gabriel Daley, the essence of Ultramontanism is 'the wish for total conformity with papal ideas and ideals in *all* things and not merely in those which are essential to the unity of the faith'. The concept was elevated to even further heights by the declaration of papal primacy and papal infallibility, and in Daley's view the Bishop of Rome became treated less as the bond of unity and charity in the Church and more as an oracular figure to be revered in his person with quasi-sacramental fervour.[17]

In the wake of the First Vatican Council, Cardinal Newman

[16] ibid., pp. 100–1.
[17] Daley, 'Faith and Theology', *The Tablet*, 18–25 April 1981, pp. 391–2.

published his *Letter to the Duke of Norfolk* to defend the Church against UK Prime Minister Gladstone's attack on papal primacy. Newman's stated view was that Catholics were bound to obey the Pope in religious matters, but they must obey the government in civil matters. He described conscience as 'the aboriginal Vicar of Christ, a prophet in its information, a monarch in its peremptoriness, a priest in its blessings and anathemas'. If, therefore, the Pope were to speak out against conscience in the true sense of the word, he would in Newman's view be cutting the ground from under his feet, 'as on the law of conscience and its sacredness are founded both his authority in theory and his power in fact'.[18]

In practice, the 90 years between the adjournment of the First Vatican Council and the start of Vatican II witnessed the emergence of an increasingly centralised and rigid Church governance, with clergy being required to take an 'anti-Modernist' oath as a precondition for ordination.[19] There was a revival of scholasticism in the form of Neo-Scholasticism and 'Thomism' – the theology of St Thomas Aquinas – became the sole criterion of theological orthodoxy. In the words of Gabriel Daley, the Church had come to resemble a village encompassed by a high wall which both protected and imprisoned the villagers, with an effective system of taboos and cautionary tales in place to discourage them from venturing beyond the wall.[20]

Vatican II signalled a change of direction for Catholic theology and ecclesiology – or, following the above analogy, 'breached the village wall in several places'. Thomism remained pre-eminent, but alternative theologies were implicitly encouraged, and local autonomy and regional diversity were acknowledged under the auspices of respective bishops who in union with the Pope were to exercise collegial responsibility for the running of the Church.

[18] John Henry Newman, quoted in Stanley L. Jaki (ed.), *Conscience and Papacy* (Real View Books, 2002), pp. 63–6.

[19] Modernism was an intellectual movement in the Church which was open to contemporary processes for elucidating the meaning of revelation, tradition, faith and dogma. See *Modern Catholic Encyclopedia*, p. 580.

[20] Daley, 'Faith and Theology', *The Tablet*, 11 April 1981, p. 361.

All the faithful, each in their own way, were understood to share in the one priesthood of Christ. The focus of authority was redirected towards service.

For some within the Church this was an exhilarating experience, but for others it was deeply disturbing to find themselves confronted by questions from which they had previously been sheltered in 'the peace, the certainties and carefully forged chain of command' of the pre-Conciliar Church. It was an environment in which problems were met not by discussion or open debate but by decree, and in which many people saw (and still do) that the distinguishing feature of their faith and Church is authority as the remedy for all uncertainty.[21]

Vatican II forcefully reaffirmed the traditional Catholic view of conscience and its crucial role in Christian moral decision-making. In the words of the 'Pastoral Constitution on the Church in the Modern World' (*Gaudium et Spes*):

> Deep within their conscience men and women discover a law which they have not laid upon themselves and which they must obey. Its voice ever calling them to love and do what is good and to avoid what is evil, tells them inwardly at the right moment: do this, shun that. For they have in their hearts a law inscribed by God. Their dignity rests in observing this law, and by it they will be judged. Their conscience is people's most secret core, and their sanctuary. There they are alone with God whose voice echoes in their depths. (*GS #16*)

What this does not explain is whether conscience can be deemed to err if God's call is directly to be heard in it. There is, of course, a personal responsibility to take the trouble to find out what is true and good rather than acting purely from blind choice or fancy, and later in the document married couples are told to

---

[21] ibid.

be ruled by conscience, but only provided this is in accord with the law of God in the teaching authority of the Church as 'the authentic interpreter of divine law' (*GS #50*). There is an element of ambiguity here which suggests conflicting views amongst the bishops that they were unable to reconcile at the time – one of the examples referred to by Pope Paul VI as 'unfinished business' that should remain open to further and deeper understanding and a variety of applications.[22]

This was quickly put to the test with the 1968 Papal Encyclical *Humanae Vitae*, which restated the Church's ban on all forms of artificial birth control. As mentioned previously, the decision was announced as 'non-infallible', but this did little to help those directly involved and gave rise to an extremely public examination of conscience by many Catholics as well as highly publicised defections from the Church. As the debate continued, the argument noticeably changed to become more an issue of authority than a matter of moral doctrine on which a majority of people seemed already to have reached their own conclusion.

The polarisation in the Church caused by *Humanae Vitae* was taken up by Bishop Butler, whose observation was that the demand for freedom frequently resulted in the right of conscience on the one hand and claims of authority on the other being canvassed with 'unparalleled vehemence'. The worry for Butler was that the exaggerations emanating from both sides could result in an assumption that conscience and authority are conflicting notions, so that one can only flourish at the expense of the other.[23]

In Butler's view, the solution was to locate and define the two notions within a proper framework on the basis that the Church cannot compel adhesion as this springs from a free and responsible act of faith by an individual. In his words, 'If I acknowledge the authority of the Church I do so by a free conscientious decision of my own and it is implied that the Church can never rightly

---

[22] Referred to by Robinson, *Confronting Power and Sex in the Catholic Church*, p. 118.

[23] Christopher Butler, *In the Light of the Council* (Darton, Longman and Todd, 1969), pp. 97–103.

order me to act against my conscience ... On the other hand, my free adhesion precisely implies the rights of the Church as my teacher and my guide.'[24]

Touching upon the distinction between infallible and non-infallible definitions, Butler saw the former as calling for an adhesion identical to one's adhesion to the Church herself, with the latter not requiring unconditional assent if serious and valid reasons exist to leave the issue open. The caution here is that a Catholic cannot simply dismiss non-infallible teachings of Popes and bishops as being of no more significance than the opinion of a private theologian.[25]

In other words, as members of the Church we begin with a spirit of wanting to believe and the will to follow what is taught, unless or until we feel unable in all conscience to continue to accept a particular precept. Speaking of non-infallible statements, Vatican II referred to a submission of the will and then the intellect to the teaching authority of the Pope (*LG* #25), but, as observed by Geoffrey Robinson, more recent documents from Rome have reversed the ordering and speak of a submission of the intellect and the will (Canon Law #752). This revision calls for an automatic intellectual assent to what is taught rather than the willingness to base this on the regard or acceptance of the person teaching. Robinson comments, 'It is the difference between a willingness to accept the Pope as a teacher and acceptance of every word the Pope teaches.'[26]

In my view, *Humanae Vitae* was a watershed in terms of Catholic perspectives on authority and conscience. The surprise at the time was the sheer scale of dissent, and for many people it was the first time they had ever even contemplated a contrary position on any Church teaching. Despite the Council's earlier and clear affirmation of the transcendent character of conscience, there seems today to be a return to an insistence on unquestioning conformity to all teaching as the litmus test of orthodoxy or loyalty. As a

---

[24] ibid.
[25] ibid.
[26] Robinson, *Confronting Power and Sex in the Catholic Church*, p. 121.

consequence, we look to be facing what Geoffrey Robinson has called 'the five vicious circles'.

1. The more a Pope insists on authority rather than persuasion, the less people listen, causing the Pope to feel the need to insist on authority.
2. The more a Pope insists on intellectual assent, the less people will be willing to accept him as teacher, causing the Pope to insist on intellectual assent to what is being taught.
3. The more insistence there is on authority, the more faith will be presented as an intellectual assent to propositions, causing more people to turn away from these propositions towards a religion of love and relationship.
4. The more people of today emphasise the individual and stress the right to their own opinion, the more a Pope will need to stress the community nature of religion, causing people to demand a more participatory community in which their opinions are listened to and taken into account.
5. The more people seek a voice in the affairs of the Church, the more a Pope can tend to turn towards a small group of 'loyal' advisors rather than seek 'the faith of the Church', as a result creating an even louder popular clamour.[27]

This is a far from encouraging scenario and in my view the exercise of authority in the Church is an increasingly pressing issue which should be high on the agenda for consideration by our pastoral leadership. Effectively, they need to find and maintain a balance in Church teaching that provides positive guidance without excess rigidity and avoids treating every question raised as a potential act of dissent that needs to be stamped out. As we

---

[27] ibid., p. 124.

are reminded by Gabriel Daley, the gospel we profess and seek to serve demands honesty, freedom and love in the way we practise, teach and explore it.[28]

To leave the last word to Bishop Butler:

> There must not be a conflict between authority and freedom in which one can only win its point at the expense of the other. Rather, there should be a dialogue of which the ultimate resolution is always left to conscience. Human responsible freedom to which the faith itself makes its appeal, is the supreme value which the Church subserves.[29]

---

[28] Daley, 'Faith and Theology', *The Tablet*, 18 April 1981, p. 446.
[29] Butler, *In the Light of the Council*, p.103.

7

The Priesthood and Pastoral Service

This two-part heading is wholly intentional, as I regard both elements to be inseparable. The former is a descriptive title or designation which finds its purpose in the latter. Treated apart, 'priesthood' can easily become both title and function for its own sake and 'pastoral ministry' lose its theological grounding.

The priesthood has always been a talking point in the Church, and for good reason. After all, it is a priest who normally baptises us into the Church, to whom we turn for Confession, who says Mass each week, who officiates at our weddings, and finally who conducts our requiem and burial. Catholic life is simply not imaginable without a priest.

My childhood parish boasted three priests. There was our long-serving parish priest and two younger curates who, following their ordination, would usually work a two- or three-year stint in several different parishes. We had shy priests, lively priests, English priests, Irish priests, nice priests, not-so-nice priests and, on (rare) occasions, not-so-very-nice-at-all priests. None of this mattered. They were all priests who had been dispatched to us to administer the sacraments.

Over the last 50 years, the number of active priests in England has reduced significantly and current statistics point to continuing reductions over the foreseeable future – a combination of the average age of existing priests and the number of new vocations. There has been a major decline in vocations over recent years and while there are reported signs of some upturn in new entries for seminary training, these are generally considered to be below the required level simply for 'net replacement'.

More than one priest per parish is now the exception, and a number of parishes are already without a full-time priest and are served by some form of 'team ministry'. Most dioceses have produced, or are in the process of drawing up, contingency plans to meet the challenge of a continuing deterioration in clergy/laity ratios and the practical implications this may pose for existing parish structures and pastoral service.

Faced with this situation, the predictable call from many quarters within the Church is for the rules to be relaxed to allow married men to be ordained, quoting the example of married ex-Anglican clergy who joined the Catholic Church in some numbers in the 1990s and who seem, for the most part, to have been well accepted. A more radical suggestion of late is for consideration to be given to the ordination of women, often accompanied by the claim that this is a matter of principle and justice as well as being supported by the fact that women account for over 50% of the Church in England and a significantly higher percentage of 'regularly practising' Catholics.

All such suggestions have been consistently dismissed by our pastoral leadership. The style of life led by Jesus is held as the example to support clerical celibacy, and his gender is given as the reason why women cannot be considered for clerical office. The issue has been officially declared a 'closed topic', with the inference being that our current hierarchical structure and model of priesthood match what was divinely instigated by Jesus and therefore we have no authority to change them. I believe the evidence of history is less convincing.

The example of Jesus

An interesting starting point is to reflect on the choice made by Jesus to be born into the tribe of Judah, 'the members of which have never done service at the altar; everyone knows he came from Judah, a tribe that Moses did not even mention when dealing with priests' (Hebrews 7:13–14). Contrast the tribe of Levi, with whom the priesthood was associated in Jewish tradition by virtue of both the law and physical descent.

It could be argued, therefore, that the priesthood of Jesus was not intended to be a continuation of this form of inherited priesthood and the whole apparatus of the 'sacral' with which it was accompanied. St Paul explains that the priesthood of Jesus is of the higher order of Melchizedek foresworn by Yahweh, and through his blameless and uncontaminated life, death and resurrection a more perfect sacrifice was offered, once and for all, and accepted by God. Jesus, now in glory, is our high priest for ever (Hebrews 7:1–28).

It is evident from the New Testament that the principal focus of Jesus' activity was the 'word' and that this took two forms: a message (*kerygma*) and an instruction (*didakhe*). In delivering the former, Jesus maintained the style of the ancient Jewish heralds or prophets, continuously moving from place to place with his message delivered and repeated to as many people and over as short a period as possible. We read that Jesus announced the nearness of the kingdom of God with a call to repent and believe in the gospel (Mark 1:14–15), that he preached this 'good news' in all Galilee (Matthew 4:23), and that his fame spread even further afield (Luke 4:14).

The 'message' was frequently taken by Jesus into the synagogue assemblies and the temple precincts, but, as observed by Jean-Paul Audet, any association with the prevailing framework of worship and the sacred which resulted from his doing so always remained with him a chance one and ultimately of secondary importance. Jesus' message was just as much at home when heard in a meeting house, in the streets and public squares, in the fields and along the wayside. Because it was everything in itself, it could be at ease in every place and circumstance and, being largely independent of cult and rite, thereby achieve the maximum flexibility and mobility.[1]

---

[1] Jean-Paul Audet, *Structures of Christian Priesthood* (Sheed & Ward Stagbooks, 1967), p. 24.

At a particular point in time, Jesus made the decision to adjust his style of approach and, as St Mark records, he began to gather round him some disciples to whom he expanded his message into formal instruction (Mark 1:16–20). For these chosen disciples, Jesus was now both herald and teacher (*didaskalos*, 'master'), and in the customary manner of master/pupil relationships in those days, their tuition is likely to have taken the form of small group sessions at which his formulae would be repeated until firmly fixed in their minds. Once memorised, a period of further explanation with questions and answers could then follow.[2]

Jesus attended his last Passover meal (the Jewish festival to celebrate God's delivery of Israel from slavery in Egypt) having booked a dining room in a private house for himself and a group of his closest disciples. At this gathering he gave them two additional instructions, both by means of example. The first was to stress the concept of service which had always been a feature of his message concerning the kingdom of God, and which he wished his disciples to continue in the future. To emphasise the point, he humbly washed the feet of those who were present (John 13:4–16).

Later, when they were at table, he undertook the blessing over the bread and the cup which he announced as being his body and blood, and which in a physical sense would shortly, and again humbly, be sacrificed on our collective behalf (Luke 22:17–20 and parallels). In continuity with the Old Testament tradition of keeping memorial, Jesus asked his disciples to continue to re-enact this new rite in his memory (Luke 22:19).

The 'Last Supper' of Jesus, conducted in the manner of the Jewish ceremony, was clearly intended to show that paschal expectations, i.e. redemption by God, would be realised through his death and resurrection. It was a 'Eucharist' (thanksgiving) that opened up new hope for all and, as St Paul would later proclaim, 'Christ our Passover has been sacrificed' (1 Corinthians 5:7).

---

[2] ibid., p. 36.

In summary, the profile of Jesus was that of a herald or prophet in the manner of the Jewish tradition. He did not seem to want to integrate his activities into the sacral apparatus of the Palestinian Judaism of his age, preferring instead to pursue a more free-ranging message and instruction, which was delivered without intent for coercion and in a genuine spirit of service. As a result of his death and resurrection he became and remains for ever our 'high priest'.[3]

The early Church

When Jesus first commissioned the Twelve, their sending out was along the same lines as his initial activity in Galilee, namely to convey a message. As recorded by St Matthew, they were told to travel light from town to town and village to village, accepting what hospitality was offered in order to proclaim that 'the kingdom of heaven was close at hand'. Included with their brief was the power to heal the sick and cast out devils, all of which came with a caution that their reception might not always be friendly and, on occasions, could even involve physical violence against them (Matthew 10:6–20).

The style of life demanded by this 'apostolic mandate' is again that of a herald or prophet, continuously on the move and by implication free from immediate family or business ties. The picture that this conveys, and certainly my original perception, is that soon after their commissioning by Jesus the apostles departed as a group, leaving all behind them, each travelling to a pre-arranged itinerary. In reality, there does not seem to have been an early or single exodus, as we read accounts of Simon, Andrew, James and John continuing to use their boats and labouring as they had done in their previous situation.[4]

It seems evident also that the service of the word in the era

---

[3] ibid., p. 23.
[4] ibid., p. 46.

of the Twelve was diverse as regards the people who took part in it, the literary form they made use of and the general conditions in which it took place. There is limited information concerning either the style or the sphere of activity of the Twelve, and of course they were not the only ones to bear the title and fill the function of 'apostle', with Paul and Barnabas as obvious additions.

In terms of the 'word', there was an undoubted continuity between the original message of Jesus and that of the apostles, but, as Jean-Paul Audet observes, we find no servile imitation of the literary forms previously adopted by Jesus and no reproduction of his individual style and in particular his use of parables.[5] The delivery process adopted by the apostles was both discursive and exhortative, as is well illustrated in the separately recorded speeches from St Peter following the outpouring of the Spirit at Pentecost (Acts 2:14–36) and from St Paul in the synagogue in Antioch (Acts 13:16–41).

These particular speeches were delivered at large public events, whereas apostolic activity tended for the most part to be directed more towards smaller gatherings, such as synagogue assemblies on the Sabbath or even smaller groups or family units where both message and instruction would have been closer to conversation than any kind of lecturing. A classic example of the latter is the invitation extended to St Peter to visit and stay at the home of the centurion Cornelius, in order for him to impart the message of the gospel and baptise the entire household together with the centurion's kinsmen and close friends (Acts 10:1–48).

This particular example begins with an invitation and an offer of hospitality in a domestic setting and serves to highlight the significance of the home in the service of the word and the early development of the Church. The pattern which began to emerge was for one or other of the Christians in a particular location to issue a welcome and lay on the hospitality in order to accommodate an 'assembly'. There is no doubting that this pastoral welcome

---

[5] ibid., p. 58.

was one of the most important functions in the service of the Church, for it was effectively this which actually re-formed the *ekklesia* (the coming together of the followers of Jesus) every time it gathered to hear the word or renew the 'Lord's Supper', or both.[6]

Moreover, an assembly within a domestic setting was readily seen and experienced as part and parcel of the rhythm of people's everyday life, rather than being an external or additional venture. The home quickly became a stable, secure and flexible base for the itinerant service of the word to continue its advance and the ideal environment in which to form the 'communion' that was the local church, which in turn would act as the leaven to attract sympathetic interest from outside and win new believers to the gospel.

The success of the domestic church did, of course, depend to a great extent on the choice of people who would extend the welcome and preside over the assemblies of the Word and Eucharist and in a general way ensure the cohesion and progress of the community in brotherly love and hope. These first 'shepherds' of the Church, the *presbyteroi* ('elders') and *episkopoi* ('superintendents'), would usually be selected from amongst those with a good reputation locally and an established record in their own households. In his letter to Timothy, St Paul wrote:

A bishop [*episkopos*] must have an impeccable manner ... must not have been married more than once ... be temperate, discreet and courteous, hospitable and a good teacher ... not a heavy drinker nor hot tempered nor a lover of money ... must manage his own family well and bring his children up to obey him and be well behaved. How can a man who does not understand how to manage his own family have responsibility for the church of God? (1 Timothy 3:4–5)

---

[6] ibid., p. 100.

In this regard, I believe there are a number of points worthy of mention. First, the several titles used in apostolic writings such as *presbyteroi, episkopoi, diakonoi* and *apostolos* all came directly from secular speech. They are not drawn from the sacral world of the Jews or even from the Greeks or Romans.

Second, those serving the gospel in the early Church did not think of themselves, nor were they thought of by the community, as being a group who formed a 'sacral caste' as, for example, would be the case for members of the Levitical priesthood. This is not to suggest that the first Christian communities dissociated themselves from the world of the sacred, but they did not extend their awareness to the point of bestowing a permanent and inalienable sacral character upon the actual persons who performed the gestures or presided over the rites.[7]

A similar attitude can be seen to have been adopted regarding the location and the furniture used for worship. It was found natural and fitting to celebrate the Eucharist in a completely social setting, namely, the homes of those who extended the welcome and hosted the occasion. After all, Jesus himself had eaten his last Passover meal in a private house and if he was content to use the table, the cups and other implements which had been provided at the time, it would be unrealistic to imagine that the early Christians would have treated their domestic implements as 'altars' or 'sacred vessels'.

The overall situation can therefore be seen as a major simplification compared with the sacral world of contemporary Judaism. This was one of the main factors that made it possible for the primitive Church to break out from the limits of Judaism so as to become part of the vast world of the Roman Empire. By lifting to some extent the burden of the sacred, the young Church gained enormous flexibility for its structures, functions and services, which for the first Christian communities assured a wide freedom of action, invention and adaptation.[8]

[7] ibid., p. 128.
[8] ibid., p. 128.

Marriage, celibacy and sex

An unmarried clergy is a recognised fact in the Catholic Church, although of late there are the examples of married ex-Anglican priests being admitted to the Catholic priesthood. We know also that ordained ministers in the Orthodox Churches below that of bishop can be married and, taken together, these two examples suggest that the issue of 'marriage and orders' is one of regulation rather than intrinsic theological opposition.

As indicated in the previous section, numerous generations in the Church lived out their Christian inheritance based on the home and the family without considering the need to extend the area of the sacred in their pastoral structures. The Church as a whole already possessed in its Eucharist a 'sacrifice of praise' (1 Peter 2:9) and believed that in Jesus, now present with his Father through his death and resurrection, it already had a 'high priest' with whose mediation no other had ever been or could ever be comparable.

By the beginning of the third century, however, Church vocabulary began to incorporate an increasing use of 'priestly' terminology alongside the earlier designations. In particular, the *presbyteroi* and *episkopoi*, because of their association with the Eucharist, became more frequently regarded as a priestly service and the sense of the sacred which is suggested by the title was extended to cover everything connected with their function, including the place of the assembly and the objects used in worship. As local Christian communities grew, they could no longer be accommodated in individual homes and specific properties were acquired for the assemblies which became treated as separate and sacred places.

A leading proponent of this understanding of the sacred was Cyprian of Carthage (d. AD 258), who defined pastoral care as first and foremost a service of the altar and sacrifices. This 'sacred ministry' became centred primarily on an altar where a sacrifice was offered, and from that centre the sacred went out to communicate itself to the pastoral world as a whole, bringing with it a sensitivity relating to the pure and the impure. Beyond the Church could now be seen a vast domain of the 'profane and the secular' with no hope of salvation, and Christian hope thus became wholly enclosed within the Church, which in its turn was wholly impregnated with a purifying atmosphere engendered by the sacred.[9]

The question at this point might well be, 'But what has this to do with marriage, celibacy and sex?' The answer can in part be traced back to the religious roots of humankind and the perceived interplay of relationships between 'the pure' and 'the sacred': the latter, with the primacy normally accorded to it in the order of values, attracts the former but excludes the possibility of contact with the impure, which is its opposite. In plain speaking, anyone who is connected in any way with the sacred must be kept a fitting distance apart from the impure, and a prime example of the impure was deemed to be the exercise of sexuality in any form.

The first official broadside in this regard came from the Council of Elvira in 306 AD. This Spanish Council proposed that married bishops, priests and deacons abstain from their wives and no longer seek to have children. This was not intended to set them free from marital cares and responsibilities, nor was it seen as the means to free them up to spend more time on pastoral activities. It was concerned solely with continence in marriage in recognition of their *sacrum ministerium*, their sacred service of the Eucharist. The punishment for non-compliance was equally straightforward, in that anyone who disobeyed would be deprived of their function.

From this beginning, the pace of 'sacralisation' continued unabated, although it is interesting to note that the ritual for the election of a bishop at this time did not describe him as sacred or consecrated, but merely as 'ordained', which had not yet come to signify consecration. This would change by the early part of the fourth century, when Eusebius of Caesarea (d. AD 340) said,

---

[9] ibid., p. 136 (note the parallel in this outlook with that of the Gnostics, referred to in Chapter 3).

'For those who have been consecrated [or made sacred] and who have engaged themselves to serve God, it is fitting to abstain afterwards from relations with their wives.'[10] The underlying view which is evident from this statement is that a recognition of the sacred would begin to draw the 'pure' into its orbit and in the eyes of many people the pure referred principally to all forms of sexual abstinence.

As this unfolding situation is described by Jean-Paul Audet, a pastoral tradition which began by being more concerned with the services than the styles of life that went with them witnessed a reversal of this order of priorities to the extent that the original styles of life themselves became thought of as appropriate 'states of life' with their own meaning and value. These states of life could therefore be idealised and subjected to stricter regulations and laws, from which it was a comparatively small step to extend a law on continence in marriage to that of total sexual continence.[11] This particular journey ended with the First and Second Councils of the Lateran (1123 and 1139), which finally declared the nullity or annulment of any marriage of a cleric in major orders.

An argument which is presented in support of this continuing Church law is that Jesus never married, thereby providing a clear indication of his intent. Indeed, the state of 'perfect and perpetual continence' is actually described in the Vatican II 'Decree on the Ministry and Life of Priests' (*Presbyterorum Ordinis* #16) as being recommended by Jesus, based on the text of Matthew 19:12. I have to admit to some difficulty with this interpretation, and all the more so when read in the extended context of Matthew 19:1–12. In any event, there can surely be no question here that Jesus was advocating a 'rule' of celibacy.

Seemingly, there is no place for any alternative explanation that, for example, Jesus might simply have decided on a style of life for himself that he considered better suited to him at the time in order to fulfil his mission. But what of the apostles? It is only

---

[10] Quoted in ibid., p. 141.
[11] ibid., p. 13.

a chance reference to Jesus visiting St Peter's mother-in-law, who was sick, that gives an indication that he was married (Matthew 8:14). For the remainder, we have no detailed information, which I interpret as meaning that their marital status was of no interest whatever to Jesus. Had this been otherwise, I would expect the Gospels to make specific reference to the fact that only single men should apply for the role.

The apostles were, of course, called upon to 'leave all' in the service of the word. But how was this understood in the language of the time and particularly by those who were married? As mentioned previously, our reading of the text today could easily be interpreted as Jesus calling for an instant and irreversible break from an earlier way of life in favour of pursuing a new and improved lifestyle, but this would seem to be a misunderstanding of the message intended by the Gospel narrators.

I believe Jesus' purpose was to make it clear that the service of the word was no sinecure. It called for a particular focus, commitment and dedication as well as a willingness to undertake regular travels, but without any definitive stipulation on the degree of 'detachment' that would be expected. This was something that was clearly considered to be a matter which could and should be worked out by each individual to depend upon their respective domestic circumstances. Thus there was no instantaneous departure of the Twelve and we find reference to apostles continuing to operate around Jerusalem (Acts 8:1) and travelling with their wives and families (Romans 16:1–16).

I imagine nevertheless that prospective recruits without marital ties or other commitments might well have been judged to be ideal candidates for the itinerant service of the word, which by its nature could suggest a single state as an advantage. In contrast, leadership of the individual local churches and the service of the assembly was born out of the wholly domestic environment of home, marriage and family in each local community, where such considerations did not apply. And yet surprisingly, this was where attitudes towards celibacy first began to change.

145

In my view, the undoubted key factor which prompted this change of attitude was a continuing confrontation in people's minds between the pure and impure, the sacred and profane – with the former in each case being associated with the service of the Eucharist and the latter with the exercise of sexuality. From this it became natural that preference should be given to what was thought to be better in itself, and predictably anything thought to be better in itself is all too likely to acquire an aura of immutability.[12]

History will attest that a dualism of this nature between the sacred and the profane was endemic in the world outside the Church, as it had been since time immemorial, but seemingly did not find a place in the pastoral consciousness of the Christian domestic assembly for more than two centuries. In due course, the pastoral desire to honour the *sacramenta* reached the point where only one possibility remained, namely, the total exclusion of the exercise of sexuality by clerics in the form of an imposed law. As a result, it can be said that the 'new priesthood' of the first generations of Christians which looked to have broken the links with Judaism began to return to rules of purity and a similar model of priesthood to the one it had originally replaced.[13]

The priesthood and pastoral service today

The Catholic priesthood is open to unmarried males who have been trained in philosophy and theology prior to being ordained. Ordination is one of the Church's seven sacraments through which the candidate receives the irrevocable power of 'Holy Orders' to officiate at the Eucharist and administer the other sacraments. The sacrament of Holy Orders is conferred by a bishop, to whom each priest is 'incardinated' (enlisted).

The first task of a priest is to preach the gospel, and for this

[12] ibid., p. ix.
[13] ibid., p. 149.

purpose he is assigned to a particular parish and will act as the personal representative of the bishop in whose diocese the parish is located. The fullness of the Catholic priesthood is vested in the bishop who, under the provisions of Canon Law (#377), is appointed by the Pope and consecrated to become 'Vicar of Christ' for all the baptised within his particular church, i.e. diocese.

Our priesthood is therefore a highly regulated and hierarchical institution which is centrally controlled from Rome and functions locally within the two administrative units of diocese and parish. The former is under the jurisdiction of the bishop, and the latter is run by the priest who is appointed by him. Generally speaking, the non-ordained faithful are members of a specific parish by virtue of where they live, and the parish church is the point of delivery for pastoral services.

As an example, the Roman Catholic Diocese of Westminster comprises most of the London boroughs north of the River Thames, together with the district of Staines and the county of Hertfordshire. The 2011 Diocesan Yearbook lists 224 parishes under the jurisdiction of an archbishop and three assistant bishops, with a total of 642 active priests to include religious congregations and societies. The parishes accommodated an average Sunday Mass attendance of 151,600 people and they were the venue for 10,176 baptisms, 1,142 marriages and 557 receptions into the Church.[14]

Statistics of this nature show the relative level of activity in each parish, and over time they can help to highlight emerging trends within a diocese. They can, of course, convey the notion of a parish as simply an operating unit which performs specified functions in a designated location. In contrast, Vatican II re-emphasised the 'community' aspect of a parish, the coming together of local congregations of the baptised whereby each local community, in the presence of Christ and through their celebration of the Eucharist, makes real the whole Church.[15] US canon lawyer James

---

[14] *Westminster Year Book 2011* (Westminster Roman Catholic Diocese Trustee © WRCDT 2010), 59th edition.
[15] *Lumen Gentium* #26.

Coriden has described this process as moving the emphasis from territory to people and from an administrative unit to a congregation of the baptised.[16]

The Vatican II 'Decree on the Church's Missionary Activity' (*Ad Gentes Divinitus*) described the formation of local churches as the work of the Holy Spirit, who in baptism begets new life to those who believe in Christ. Gathered as a community, they become a sign of God's presence in the world (*AG* #15). In its theology of the parish, the Council also emphasised that the threefold office of Christ, that of priest, prophet and king, was a shared responsibility of all the faithful, with pastoral ministry a community responsibility.[17] As this was described by Pope John Paul II in an address to bishops in 1986, 'The parish itself is the active subject of pastoral action ... it is the parish which renders the mystery of the church and of its mission living and operative.'[18]

The community aspect of a parish is now enshrined in the 1983 Code of Canon Law, namely, 'a definite community of the Christian faithful established on a stable basis within a particular church; the pastoral care of the parish is entrusted to a pastor as its own shepherd under the authority of the diocesan bishop' (#515.1). As further explained by James Coriden, the choice of words in this definition is deliberate. In particular, 'community' signifies that a parish is more than a territory or simply a gathering of people, as it involves individuals and families who know each other, worship together and share common values and interests.

The word 'definite' means that the community is designated in some way to a particular area and 'established on a stable basis' indicates that a parish is not a one-time gathering, a temporary assembly or convention. People may leave or be replaced by others over time, but the intention of the members of the community is permanence rather than transience. The term 'within a particular church' places each parish in a diocese, and 'under the authority

---

[16] James Coriden, *The Parish in Catholic Tradition* (Paulist Press, 1997), p. 47.

[17] 'Decree on the Apostolate of the Lay People', *Apostolicam Actuositate, AA* #10.

[18] Referred to by Coriden, *The Parish in Catholic Tradition*, p. 92.

of the diocesan bishop' signifies one of the bonds that link each local church within a diocesan communion and at the same time reflects a function of the bishop's supervisory role in appointing parish priests.

'Pastoral care' for the parish is shown to be entrusted to a parish priest with the normal arrangement being for each community to have its own resident pastor. The Code also specifies or implies many activities that are obligatory or at least appropriate for parishes and, while often stated in terms of being the duties of the pastor, they do involve and affect the entire community. These include the proclamation of the word of God, catechesis, worship of God centred on the Eucharist, sacramental celebrations, prayers, works of penance, caring for community members, promoting family life, witness to social justice, and mission outreach to spread the gospel message.

First and foremost, then, a parish needs to be seen as a human community gathered together in faith. Community in this context is understood as a group of individuals and families who, for the most part, live in close proximity, know each other, share common values and relate with one another. Members of such a community are interactive and realise their interdependence in living out their religious lives. They worship together, grow in the faith together and face the crises of life together. They join in celebrating family births and baptisms, marriages and funerals. There are multiple bonds between them.[19]

This is very much how I imagine it would have been with the Christian communities in the apostolic era: groups of families who had become Christians and judged this to be the driving force in their lives, who met regularly for worship and helped one another to create a vibrant and supportive 'Christian environment' which continued to attract new followers from the wider neighbourhood. So what of our present situation? Does this description reflect the generally held view of what parish life today is all about? And if not, what can we do to rectify the situation?

---

[19] ibid., pp. 59–63.

In answer to the first part of the question, I suspect that many of us may have a more detached involvement. We reside within a definable parish boundary and we know the Mass times at our local church in order to fulfil our Sunday obligations. From time to time we may support other parish functions of a religious or social nature and we possibly know a number of other Catholics by sight who happen to live in our immediate vicinity, have children at the same local school or perhaps regularly attend the same Mass.

In other words, we can tend to function as individual Catholics or Catholic families who belong to a parish community in the sense of 'community' being a collective noun rather than the description of a concept. As indicated previously, a parish might be judged principally by reference to Mass numbers or the range of events and activities which are organised on a regular basis, but this need not be indicative of the level of success in achieving what I would regard as its principal goal, namely, the building up of a genuine and cohesive Christian community – a community of evangelisers and a leaven for the wider society.

The 'common good' of the local church has been described by the canonist James Provost as 'the sum of those conditions which are necessary so that each Catholic may truly hear and follow the call of Christ'.[20] Mass is obviously at the heart of this and other activities will play their part, but if these events become an end in themselves they can divert attention from their real aim of helping us to develop as a more focused and committed group of followers of Jesus.

The call by Vatican II for greater lay participation has undoubtedly produced results, but this can vary from parish to parish and effectively hinges on the attitude of the individual parish priest. Indeed, the whole well-being of the parish lies very much in the hands of the incumbent pastor (echo the view of St Paul mentioned previously) and a frequent cause of tension can be the arrival of

[20] James Provost, 'Promoting and Protecting the Right of Christians', *The Jurist*, 1986, p. 283.

a new pastor who wishes to introduce sweeping changes to existing practices. This is not to question his canonical right to do so, but more a case of how he sets about explaining (or not) and implementing these changes. One sometimes wonders if any attention is given to the development of 'people skills' as part of the seminary curriculum!

A 1990 study by the Jesuit sociologist Joseph Fichter divided a typical parish (based on a US model) into four categories of parishioner. The first category is the 'nuclear', which comprises the most active and loyal parishioners and possibly accounts for 5%, or at the very most 10%, of total recorded attendees. The second category is the 'modal', which includes those who are fairly regular participants on Sundays and holidays but possibly not greatly involved in other activities and may account for up to a further 70% of the total. The next category is the 'marginal', those whose observance is infrequent but who are at least known and seen on occasions. The final category is the 'lapsed', those who may well be recorded on parish baptismal records but at some time in the past have ceased to practise and to all intents and purposes appear to have no interest in resuming parish life.[21]

I imagine that similar ratios could apply in most English parishes and no doubt with a continuing trend for the 'marginal' category to increase at the expense of the 'modal' category. I suspect that our 'lapsed' category could now account for well over 50% of originally baptised Catholics, involving a wide cross section of ages, and we might now consider introducing a further category, namely, the growing number of children of lapsed parents who have never even been presented for baptism in the first place and for whom we have no record.

These are depressing figures and in part I believe they reflect some of the major sociological changes which have occurred over the last 60 years. The 'extended family' in one particular location is no longer a norm and the local parish church may not be the

---

[21] Referred to by Coriden, *The Parish in Catholic Tradition*, p. 6.

automatic, central point of focus for Catholics living in a particular district. They will have become more affluent and mobile with easy access to a whole range of other social and cultural activities and may possibly find Mass times and the order of service in other parishes better suited to their busy weekly schedules and individual preferences. Behavioural mores in society are less rigid and censorial than in the past and people need to be helped to remain enthusiastic followers. The practice of religion has become just one pursuit which competes for people's time and attention.

An example of the Church's difficulty is given by the historian Stephen Clark, in that despite the many improved educational methods and aids which are now at our disposal, the impact of Catholic education and publications such as a catechism was probably greater 30 years ago. At that time there was an environmental dynamic for some form of institutionally directed religious education, whereas significantly less value is now placed on organised religion or on living as Christians, and this will limit both the thrust and the benefit of any educational programme, however well designed. The answer, in Clark's view, is that such programmes need to be part of a broader initiative which seeks to reinstate a Christian environment.[22]

A Christian environment requires that Christianity be part of the way that people voluntarily interact; they have to be motivated to talk about it in a way that shows they consider it important and accepted, and to behave in their daily lives and relationships in a manner that shows it is of value to them and that others can witness.[23] It seems to me that we need to recapture something of the vitality and common purpose which I remember from the parish community of my youth, but adapting our approach to accommodate the different priorities, sensitivities and general changes that are a feature of our contemporary social environment.

---

[22] Stephen Clark, *Building Christian Communities* (Ave Maria Press, 1972), p. 38.
[23] ibid., p. 32.

Looking to the future

I believe it is possible to identify some parallels between our current situation and that of the early Church. First, there is an atmosphere of suspicion and even a degree of hostility in some quarters to the Christian message, although I suspect that today it could be more a case of indifference to what is perceived as the value and function of the Church. Second, our society has also devised and follows numerous gods, be they money, power or pleasure, with transitory cults and causes continuing to emerge that capture people's imagination for a time until something new comes along.

Clearly, the lifestyle of first-century Palestine bears little relationship to twenty-first-century Britain, but I believe we might usefully consider some of the constitutive elements that enabled Christian communities to come into existence and sustain their vitality. I believe these might be summarised as an all-inclusive welcome and the resultant feeling of belonging in a community with like attitudes towards friendship and concern for others, an abiding sense of Jesus' presence in his Word and Eucharist and the desire to live and promote these values.

Welcome and belonging

A feeling of being welcome and of belonging meets a human need which applies to every generation in every place. It underscores the fact that we are social beings, we are relationship orientated, we need to be together with others in order to function well. This is even more applicable in a Christian context, where we are called to become a people who are 'not strangers or sojourners' but a community 'built on the foundation of the apostles and prophets with Jesus as the cornerstone in whom the whole structure is joined together and grows into a holy temple in the Lord' (Ephesians 1:9–12; 2:19–22).

The aim of any pastoral initiative should therefore be to create a community that people make a conscious decision to join and are enthusiastic to continue as active participants along with others who are similarly motivated. This was certainly true in the early years of the Church, but as Christianity became the religion of the state and the Church its religious institution, to be a member of society and a member of the Church was effectively the same thing. People were not called upon to make a personal choice and commitment in quite the same way.[24]

We have now perhaps run full circle and to be a Christian again requires a purposeful choice to be made and honoured. Do we look to be an inviting group of people for others to want to join us? Do new arrivals in our parishes receive a personal welcome and follow up? Can we explain why we are Catholics and do the things we do? Is it evident from what we say and do that we are followers of Jesus, and does our 'seven days a week' lifestyle match the precepts we profess on Sundays? The answer to these and other similar questions could reveal a disparity between individual parishes, but at least asking the questions is a good starting point, rather than simply relying on statistics as a standard measure of progress to be applied in the same way to evaluate every parish.

Over recent years, a significant new factor affecting established parish structures and activities has been the massive influx of migrants from widely differing cultural backgrounds, many knowing little English. We like to refer to ourselves as a 'global Church' and we are now being called upon to live up to this, as many of the new arrivals naturally seek out and expect our domestic Catholic institutions to help them continue to follow their faith. How accommodating have we been in responding to new arrivals on this scale, which has dramatically changed the demographics of many of our existing parishes?

It is evident that new arrivals on this sort of scale can give rise to tensions at parish level and create a situation that calls for pastoral support for both the indigenous and the new congregations.

---

[24] ibid., p. 41.

What is not so evident is a clear and cohesive policy from our pastoral leadership to deal with the spiritual and practical issues involved with this degree of movement and required assimilation. The principal Catholic influx into England to date has been from Poland, and the Polish bishops seem to wish to retain control over 'their' congregations both liturgically and theologically. How far is ethnic separation to be taken and for how long should it apply in this form? Some agreed future strategy by the respective bishops is surely necessary.

The liturgy of the Word and the Eucharist

Vatican II described the liturgy as the summit towards which the activity of the Church is directed and the source from which all its power flows (*SC* #10). Central to this is our weekly assembly when we come together as a single people to listen to the Word of God and share in the Eucharist of his Son with Jesus being present amongst us. The early Church was well aware of this continuing presence of Jesus and successfully integrated his message within their existing Jewish traditions, thereby expanding and enhancing the whole import of the Word of God.

For my generation I believe that attitudes in respect of weekly Mass attendance continue to some extent to be functional – a product of the Church's compulsory requirement to keep Sundays holy by hearing Mass and resting from servile work.[25] To 'hear Mass' is still an expression we use and for my generation involved little more than this, namely, to be physically present at the ceremony and listen to what was said. Seemingly this is no longer judged by younger generations to be a sufficiently convincing reason for them to commit to the same regular compliance.

When people say, 'I must go to Mass,' it is usually taken to mean that they must go in order to fulfil an obligation. Why can it not mean, 'I must go, because it is an event which I simply

---

[25] *Penny Catechism* #230.

do not wish to miss'? Why can it not be seen as an opportunity to take an active part at a regular celebration in the company of Jesus and one's fellow Christians?

Vatican II called for the faithful to participate actively in the Mass, having been made fully aware of what was involved. The Mass is considered further in the next chapter, but as regards its place at the heart of our Catholic faith, I believe we still have some way to go in order to achieve the degree of knowledge, appreciation and enthusiasm which was hoped for by the Council Fathers.

The Council also sought to promote a greater appreciation of Scripture within the Church, but in my view the general level of understanding remains limited in terms of the use of story, myth and symbolism as the means of highlighting its true content and continuing relevance. For many people there is an ever-present risk that every narrative will be treated literally and this can so often create apparent but wholly unnecessary conflicts with the fruits of modern scientific, philosophical and even biblical scholarship.

Care and support

Our primary purpose as 'Church' is to give praise and glory to God as a people united with Jesus on a journey towards our ultimate destiny of being with God. The care and support of others is an obvious and automatic by-product of this imperative, based on the words and actions of Jesus, and this was well understood and implemented in the early Church. Each community is recorded as pooling their resources and forming special 'ministries' to care for widows, orphans and the sick when the need arose. Christians in this period quickly developed a reputation as people who were seen to genuinely love and care for one another.

Much of what has developed from this earlier Christian outreach has become the responsibility of civil society, or falls under the generic heading of 'charity', covering a broad range of causes and involving many different religious and single-issue organisations. It can also be described as big business, which is not intended to detract from the benefits it generates, but unlike the response made by the early Christian communities, an involvement for us today can easily be confined to arm's-length cash contributions.

A pertinent question for us today is whether present society sees us as people who love and care for each other and whether we extend this outside our immediate communities. Do we deserve such a description from the way we are seen to respond generally to our claimed Christian precepts? I suspect that we could and should do more, with a particular focus on the 'human touch' when dealing with calls for help and understanding, and with a willingness to devote time and effort to meet such calls rather than simply offering anonymous financial donations. The parable of the 'good Samaritan'(Luke 17:11–19) should always remain an inspiration.

We can, of course, be proud of the daily and often unsung support and compassion provided through numerous Church agencies throughout the world, whose focus is on the immediate needs of individuals and groups of people rather than simply promoting causes. We need to find ways to replicate this in our own domestic situation and perhaps a good starting point could be the way in which we respond to the current needs and aspirations of fellow Catholics and indeed all other migrants seeking to join our local communities.

By way of summary, we have a shortage of priests in the English Church and for the foreseeable future the situation can only become worse. This will affect the functionality of parishes as they are presently constituted and in my view this is an opportune moment to review the whole topic of the 'Christian community' in our contemporary environment, rather than confining ourselves to piecemeal adjustments of existing institutional structures.

In light of current demographics, we should be asking ourselves what the real needs are, and considering the range of possibilities for the delivery of pastoral services that help to strengthen and expand our local communion of churches in order to produce a vibrant Christian witness. How are today's base communities best composed and formed? How do we ensure the optimum levels of inclusivity? Is there an ideal size of community, and by reference to what criteria in different places and situations? Who should be responsible and accountable for which functions? The custom of the early Church was to adapt the assembly to the inherent possibilities of the form of worship rather than insisting upon conformity to a single model of assembly. There must be a lesson here for us today.

In terms of priesthood in the Church, Jesus entrusted his 'memorial' to a purposely chosen group of twelve apostles, but without issuing a definitive job specification. This would be for them and their successors to develop based on his teachings and life example, with the promise that his Spirit would accompany all their endeavours. As a result, I seriously question the way our current model of priesthood is frequently presented, as if it is the exact and only valid version of what Jesus intended and must, as a result, be preserved without change for all time. If nothing else, this is dishonest.

We seem to have become more concerned with the style of life and state of life relating to the priesthood rather than with its underlying purpose in building up the people of God. Clearly, it would be naïve to imagine that a global Church of more than a billion souls could function without any formal structures and an obvious chain of command, but we could do well to remember that the form in which this has evolved over nearly 2,000 years owes as much to organic, circumstantial and political factors as it does to theological considerations. In the final analysis the criterion by which it must be judged is the effectiveness of its service to the people of God in each successive generation.

8

The Mass

On a recent visit to Gatwick airport I was both surprised and heartened to hear the public announcement that a Catholic Mass was about to begin and everyone was welcome. I was surprised because this is England and, more to the point, politically correct England where a 'promotion' of this sort might be judged to favour Catholics at the expense of other faith groups. It was heartening nevertheless to know that there would be a Mass in the hustle and bustle of a busy international airport and that a 'Catholic Mass' was presumed to need no further explanation.

So has the Mass become a recognised feature of contemporary English life? I guess it possibly has to the extent that the word is frequently heard in use by Catholics, it appears in the press, there are Masses which are televised for the Sunday 'religious slot' and Mass times can be seen displayed on boards outside Catholic churches in most countries around the world. But how to describe the Mass other than simply as a religious service for Catholics? This could be an altogether different issue and one which I suspect may represent something of a challenge even for people within the Church.

Referring yet again to my *Penny Catechism*, the Mass is described there as the sacrifice of the body and blood of Jesus Christ, really present on the altar under the appearances of bread and wine when offered to God for the living and the dead (#277). It is the same sacrifice as that of the cross, in which Jesus continues to offer himself in an un-bloody manner on the altar through the ministry of his priests (#278). The Mass is offered to give supreme honour and glory to God, to thank him for our benefits, to satisfy him for our sins and to obtain the grace of repentance as well as all other graces and blessings through Jesus (#279).

These are succinct and accurate responses of the sort we were frequently called upon to memorise as children, which provided ready answers but were a little light on explanations. For many people this may well be the only descriptions of the Mass they have ever received, but in the years before Vatican II this would not have been a cause for concern. We had a 'set piece' Mass, which was led exclusively by the priest and which for the most part was conducted in silence. Our involvement was totally passive and it was assumed that this was how the Mass had always been and how it was always meant to be. Small wonder that the changes which came about as a result of Vatican II gave rise to a mixture of confusion, concern and discontent.

Unfortunately, nobody at the Council appears to have been charged with the responsibility to prepare the faithful for the changes which would occur. For some people, any change was regarded as an interference with a divine inheritance, or an intrusion into their personal realm of piety. Others welcomed the increased use of English and an opportunity for greater participation, but from my recollection at the time the arguments for and against were mainly confined to the external form and shape of the ceremony. The emphasis which the Council Fathers had placed on explaining the nature and purpose of the various elements of the Mass seemed to have been overlooked or ignored.

More than 40 years and two generations later, I am not sure whether we have made much progress in this regard. There is a sizeable grouping within the Church whose allegiance to the 'old Mass' appears undiminished and which no doubt received a major boost with the recent *moto proprio* from Pope Benedict XVI proposing the reinstatement of a specific form of Latin Mass.[1] By contrast, the majority of the 'over 50s' have by now become

---

[1] *Sumarorem Pontificam*, 2007.

accustomed to the post-Conciliar liturgy, although I suspect with widely varying degrees of enthusiasm. For those who are younger, this is the only form of the Mass they have ever experienced and the level of regular attendance within the 18–30 age group is perhaps indicative of their general verdict.

Still today, the focus of attention and debate is mainly directed towards the externals of the ceremony rather than encouraging a better understanding and appreciation of the Mass itself. Why do we come together in this way on a regular basis? What is it in which we are participating and what does this participation actually achieve? Even in respect of the externals, there appear to be conflicting assertions on the origins and importance of particular elements that continue to perpetuate misunderstandings. In my opinion, a comprehensive educational programme on the Mass for adult Catholics is long overdue and is yet another priority which our pastoral leadership needs to address. Below is my brief introduction to the process.

The example of Jesus

The Mass was instigated by Jesus at the 'Last Supper', on the eve of his passion and death. The event is recorded in the Gospels of St Matthew, St Mark and St Luke, although the first written testimony came from St Paul, in his letter to the Corinthians which appeared about 20 years after the actual event. His description of the proceedings and his choice of words will therefore have been based on earlier oral testimony which already existed within the Christian community.

As described by St Paul, Jesus took some bread, thanked God for it and broke it, as he said, 'This is my body which is for you; do this as a memorial of me.' In the same way, he took the cup after supper and said, 'This cup is the new covenant in my blood. Whenever you drink it do this as a memorial of me' (1 Corinthians 11:23–25).

161

In his book *The Story of the Mass*, Pierre Loret contrasts the variations between this version of St Paul and those of the other evangelists, which he sees as sharing a fidelity to the meaning of the words Jesus used without 'slavish literalness'. In Loret's view, Jesus did not utter words for them to be repeated as if they were a magic formula which had come down from heaven. His words expressed his intent. If he had wanted to pass on a strict literal transcript, he would have said so at the time and we would presumably still be celebrating the Mass in Aramaic.[2]

So what is Jesus proposing here? To begin with, it is necessary to appreciate the symbolism of bread and wine in the Jewish tradition. From the earliest times these elements were offered in sacrifice as a grateful acknowledgement of the goodness of creation. Unleavened bread and a 'cup of blessing' later acquired added significance and formed part of the yearly Passover celebration to mark the Exodus, the liberation of Israel from slavery in Egypt and the fulfilment of God's promise.

The same elements of bread and wine were at the heart of Jesus' Passover celebration and he too began by giving thanks to God. He then proceeded to introduce a profoundly new dimension, whereby at his word the bread and wine were transformed into his body and blood – the body and blood that would shortly be sacrificed on the cross to achieve our liberation from the slavery of sin.

Once again, we need to consider Jesus' words and intentions in the Jewish context of the time. In our contemporary language, to talk of bread becoming a person's body sounds incredible and to talk of eating a person's body and drinking their blood seems repulsive because the individual words have a particular meaning for us. By contrast, the Hebrew understanding of 'body' did not just mean the physical or visible part of a person, but more what the person actually *is*. In our vocabulary, the word 'body' might be more akin to describing someone's 'personality'.[3]

---

[2] Pierre Loret, *The Story of the Mass* (Liguori Publications, 1982), p. 12.
[3] Paul McPartlan, *Eucharist: The Body of Christ* (Catholic Truth Society, 2004), p. 23.

By the same token, the life of all creatures was seen in the Old Testament as being in the blood (Leviticus 17:11), and as life comes from God, blood was sacred, the very symbol of life. As a consequence, it was permissible to eat the flesh of animals but never their blood, and blood which was shed from animal sacrifices offered in the Temple was seen to symbolise the self-offering of the person making the sacrifice – an act of dedicating their own lives to God.[4]

The Passover celebration of Jesus was therefore a thanksgiving (the Greek word being *eukaristein*, hence 'Eucharist') and at the same time a self-offering of his life to his Father. By inviting his disciples to eat the bread and wine which he had changed into his body and blood, he thereby made them participants in this whole movement of self-offering, irretrievably united to Jesus and to each other. In the words of Paul McPartlan, when Jesus says, 'This is my body,' he means, 'This is myself, my whole being,' which he gives to them so that they, by receiving, will be drawn into his own self-gift to his Father and to each individual. When he says, 'This is my blood,' he means, 'This is myself, my very life,' the life God gave him and which he in turn is giving to them so that his life might be in them and they, in him, might dwell in God.[5]

This is a truly astounding concept which we can only begin to understand as a 'mystery' and for which we must remain ever grateful as the recipients and beneficiaries of this privilege. As described by St Paul, it is God's plan to sum up all things in Jesus, to unite Jews and Gentiles through the cross so as to form a new person and reconcile them both to God (Ephesians 1 – 3). And again, the mystery which was hidden for generations is 'Christ among you, your hope of glory, that all may be made perfect in him' (Colossians 1:27).

Jesus then went on to propose that his disciples should repeat

---

[4] ibid., p. 24.
[5] ibid., p. 24.

this celebration themselves in his memory, introducing yet another biblical thread. 'Memorial' in this sense was not simply to recollect a past event, but by and through its liturgical celebration to make the event present and real. Thus every time the Jewish Passover was celebrated the Exodus events were made present in the memories of the believers so that they might conform their lives to them. In the same way, to celebrate the Eucharist not only recalls the events that saved us, but repeats them. As this is described in the *Catechism*, 'The sacrifice of the cross is *re-presented* (made real) because it is its *memorial* and because it *applies* its fruit' (#1365).

In summary, Jesus followed the ancient ritual of thanksgiving and sacrifice offered by Israel as the people of God's initial covenant and then proceeded to give it a fundamentally new and definitive form to apply henceforth. As this is further expressed in the *Catechism*, the sacrifice of Jesus on the cross and the sacrifice of the Eucharist are one single sacrifice, only the manner of offering is different (#1367). His once-and-for-all sacrifice on the cross remains ever present at each celebration of his Passover (#1364), 'and we, the body of Christ, participate in this offering of our head' (#1368).

The apostolic liturgy

The coming of the Holy Spirit at Pentecost transformed the apostles and in full 'pro-active' mode they set about proclaiming that Jesus was our only salvation (Acts 2). They had witnessed their Master's Passover meal and received his instruction to 'do this' as a memorial. But what did *this* actually entail? Was it a celebration they should hold once a year to coincide with the Passover festivities? Should it always form part of a meal? Was there a rhythm or ceremonial pattern that they were expected to follow? Was it to be conducted in Aramaic? What should it be called?

These and other issues had to be resolved by the apostles, who were forced to rely on their collective experience and judgement at the time. After all, there were no priests, Levites or leaders of the synagogue amongst them able to provide a 'professional' input. Their individual experience up to that point was likely to have been confined to presiding over Passover celebrations in the home or at family meals on the Sabbath which had a religious orientation.

From the outset there was an ongoing liturgical association with the synagogue, just as there had been with Jesus during his lifetime. Typically, the apostles and their recent converts would participate in the readings and prayers and then return home in order to 'break bread', which in the early years would almost certainly have taken place during a meal. This second 'domestic liturgy' would have been without the time-honoured prescriptions which governed proceedings in the Temple, but over time various liturgical habits and rituals began to evolve. St Paul in particular took a lead in seeking to highlight what he considered to be the appropriate words, actions and general demeanour that should be adopted in the Christian assembly (1 Corinthians 11:1–33).

A number of years later, Christians were formally barred from attending the synagogue, but because of the importance they attached to their scriptural heritage, the readings from the Law and the Prophets were incorporated into their domestic liturgy, together with further readings based on accepted testimonies concerning Jesus. Thereafter, the Christian assembly comprised a 'liturgy of the Word' and a 'liturgy of the Eucharist', with both elements maintaining a close association with their Jewish roots.

The weekly readings and the prayers which had been taken from the Old Testament were now seen as being fulfilled in Jesus. The bread and wine were understood as a true sacrificial meal that enabled those present to be sharers in the original sacrifice of the cross, having as its source the Jewish *Zebah Todah* (*Zebah*, 'sacrifice'; *Todah*, 'communion') which had traditionally been offered in the Temple.[6]

---

[6] Loret, *The Story of the Mass*, p. 25.

There were, of course, a number of departures from original Jewish practices. The day for the Christian assembly was moved from Saturday as the last day of the week (Sabbath) to Sunday – the day of Jesus' resurrection and the day on which he again shared a meal with his disciples. The use of Greek became widespread at the weekly assembly as the language spoken by most of the early converts, acknowledging the necessity for there to be an intelligible medium of communication during this formative period.

By the end of the apostolic era and moving into the second century, a basic line for the order of the eucharistic celebration had begun to emerge. Quoting from the writings of St Justin Martyr (d. c. AD 165), the *Catechism* states:

On the day we call the day of the sun, all who dwell in the city or country gather in the same place. The memoirs of the apostles and the writings of the prophets are read as much as time permits.

When the reader has finished, he who presides over those gathered, admonishes and challenges them to imitate these beautiful things.

Then all rise together and offer prayers for ourselves and for all others, wherever they may be, so that we may be found righteous by our life and actions ... and faithful to the commandments, so as to obtain eternal salvation.

When the prayers are concluded we exchange the kiss.

Then someone brings bread and a cup of water and wine mixed together to him who presides over the brethren.

He takes them and offers praise and glory to the Father of the universe through the name of the Son and of the Holy Spirit and for a considerable time he gives thanks that we have been judged worthy of these gifts.

When he has concluded the prayers and the people have responded, those whom we call deacons present the 'Eucharisted' bread, wine and water and take them to those who are absent. (#1345)

It is clear from this account that much of the sequence of our present Mass was already operative at this early stage. Notable omissions are a formal Credo (which would not become a regular feature of the Roman liturgy until the eleventh century) or any example of a specific prayer to offer praise and glory to God. The very good reason for this was that there was no 'authorised text' in existence at this point. The celebrants of the Eucharist were free, within limits, to compose their own prayers and organise the ritual.

The ceremony concluded with those who were well to do and willing giving what donation each thought fit. What was collected was deposited with the president, who succoured the orphans and widows and those who through sickness or any other cause were in want.

The development of the eucharistic liturgy

It will be evident from the foregoing that the apostles did not receive a ready-made eucharistic liturgy and it is equally the case that there was no apostolic liturgy *per se* from which all later ones would derive. The task for the Church (then and now) is to preserve the essentials of Jesus' mandate while giving suitable form and expression to its enactment in each ensuing age.

During the first millennium the Christian communities had to contend with all manner of issues, ranging from state persecution to internal heresies, as well as the political upheavals following the break-up of the Roman Empire and the social implications of migration involving diverse peoples, languages and cultures. In the words of Pierre Loret, improvisation in liturgy at this time tended to be the rule rather than the exception.[7]

The second millennium witnessed a serious theological split (with political undertones) between the Latin (Roman Catholic)

---

[7] ibid., p. 40.

Church in the West and the Greek (Orthodox) Church in the East. This did not undermine the common understanding of the nature and purpose of the Eucharist, but a change in emphasis developed over the years in certain areas, most notably the role of the Holy Spirit. Following a further split in the Western Church as a result of the sixteenth-century Protestant Reformation, a highly structured liturgical form was introduced as the sole authorised model for the Eucharist for Roman Catholics and conformity to this was rigidly enforced over the next 400 years, virtually up to the start of Vatican II.

It is beyond the scope of this book to attempt to provide a blow-by-blow account of 2,000 years of development of the liturgy, and I propose merely to highlight a number of the events and circumstances which I consider pertinent to the way in which we perceive and celebrate Mass today.

Why the name 'Mass'?

As a starting point, why is it called 'Mass?' The word itself appears to have emerged from a general usage amongst the faithful, but was not officially adopted until around the fifth century. Derived from the Latin *misa*, meaning 'dismissal', it seems an improbable choice of title as it says nothing about the eucharistic mystery. Its use was to announce that the ceremony was over: 'you are dismissed' – *ita misa est*. Nonetheless, this is the name that has endured up to the present time, although following Vatican II the word 'Eucharist' has perhaps begun to regain some of its former standing.

Language

The language of literature and culture in the Roman Empire was Greek. The Gospels were written in Greek and this became the language used for the readings at the weekly liturgy. However, at the beginning of the third century, Pope Callistus introduced Latin into the liturgy on behalf of the growing numbers of the faithful living in Rome who did not speak Greek. His decision was not universally popular and generated serious dissent, with the complete 'Latinisation' of the liturgy in Rome taking almost 150 years to achieve.[8]

Latin had been the language of administration throughout the Empire and continued to be a convenient means of communication with and between the numerous different tribes who had begun to settle across Europe in the aftermath their earlier invasions. A Latin liturgy was an obvious export from Rome for the Church in the West, whereas with less centralised ecclesial authority in the East a greater linguistic diversity continued. Centuries later, the irony for us is that what began as a means for the faithful to understand and participate at Mass eventually became a language which few people other than clerics continued to use or even understand.

Early liturgies

The bishops of the Church had always assumed the right to improvise their own prayers for the liturgy, but from the third century onwards specific examples of eucharistic prayers began to emerge and ultimately became recommended material for general use. One of the earliest examples is found in the manuscript known as the *Apostolic Succession* and attributed to the priest Hyppolytus from around AD 215. This provides an account of the liturgy and the organisation of the early Church by means of a description of the ceremony for the ordination of a bishop where the text is unmistakably the foundation of what is now our Second Eucharistic Prayer.[9]

A later composition attributed to St Ambrose of Milan (d. AD 397) includes a prayer which is virtually word for word what eventually

---

[8] ibid., p. 40.
[9] ibid., p. 38.

became the 'Roman Canon' and which we now refer to as the First Eucharistic Prayer. The term 'canon' comes from the Latin for 'rule' and in respect of the Mass this meant a prayer that the celebrant was obliged to say without changing anything in it. This particular dictate was introduced at the beginning of the fifth century at the behest of Pope Innocent I, and so this version of the eucharistic prayer became 'the rule' for Rome.[10]

Special mention should also be made of St Gregory (d. AD 604) who, following his election as Pope in 590, compiled the forerunner of our present missal. This involved condensing several earlier books together with corrections and clarifications which were undertaken in a manner which has been described as 'with due Roman moderation'. However, Gregory's works did not pass without criticism and he was accused of tampering with the 'apostolic prayer', to which his response was that there had never been such a prayer to begin with and that the mediocre scholarship of many of the texts which were in use made improvements essential.[11]

It is important to record that despite the patronage of several successive Popes, the 'Roman liturgy' remained relatively local for some time in its use and application. Liturgical diversity remained a feature of the wider Church within Europe and was considered both the norm and the preference for most people. Throughout the Middle Ages there was very much a two-way dialogue between Rome and other liturgical traditions and the Roman liturgists of the time seemed well aware that their 'indigenous formula' could not simply be imposed, but required adaptation before adoption in order for people to see that what was being presented was a reflection of their own tastes and customs.[12]

Perhaps this is a policy which Rome might again like to consider for present application!

---

[10] ibid., p. 53.
[11] ibid., p. 52.
[12] ibid., p. 68.

'The body of Christ'

'The body of Christ' and 'the mystical body of Christ' are expressions which we hear on a regular basis. The former is pronounced at every Mass when the consecrated host is offered to each individual, and the Church is frequently referred to as the mystical body of Christ. No apparent issue here, except that this is a reversal of how these expressions were used and understood by Christians for over a thousand years.

At his Passover celebration Jesus took bread and wine and declared, 'This is my body ... This is my blood ... Do this as a memorial.' The symbolism of the bread and wine will not have been lost on the apostles as a result of their common Jewish heritage and they will have been left in little doubt of Jesus' clear intent to become *truly* present in some mysterious manner in these elements. In the words of Paul McPartlan, it follows that the Eucharist is, technically speaking, the mystical body of Christ, which literally just means the body of Christ present under the signs and symbols of the Church's sacramental life – in this case in the form of bread and wine.[13]

The apostles will also have been aware of a wider significance which was implicit in Jesus' words and actions, as highlighted by St Paul when he spoke of our forming a single body because we partake in this one loaf (1 Corinthians 10:16–17). The same connection was made by St Cyprian (d. AD 258), who said:

For when the Lord calls his body the bread which is made up of many grains joined together, he means by that the union of all Christian people which he contained within himself. And when he calls his blood the wine which is made into one drink of many grapes, he again means that the flock which we form is made up of individuals who have regained their unity.[14]

---

[13] McPartlan, *Eucharist: The Body of Christ*, p. 48.
[14] Referred to by Henri deLubac, *Catholicism: Christ the Common Destiny of Man* (Ignatius Press, 1988), p. 90.

For St Augustine, Christ and the Church were judged inseparable and formed what he termed the *totus Christus,* the whole Christ, head and members, so to receive the body of Christ is in fact to be received by him into his body which is the Church. In other words, the body of Christ which we take into ourselves actually takes us out of ourselves into the communion of the Church. As he famously expressed it in one of his sermons, ' "The body of Christ" you are told and you answer "Amen". Be members then of the body of Christ that your Amen may be true.'[15]

The unmistakable testimony of these early Christian leaders is that the body of Christ is the Church. Jesus is the head and we are the members living out God's plan in unity with him and with each other, a family of local churches, a communion of communions until we finally (and hopefully) all become the heavenly community. Meantime, the place where we most fully enter into this great historical plan is in the celebration of the Eucharist, or as so profoundly expressed by the twentieth-century theologian Henri deLubac, 'The Eucharist makes the Church.'[16]

So why did a change occur in the use and understanding of these two expressions? This can be traced to the twelfth century when (not for the first time) doubts were expressed as to whether Jesus was *really* present in the sacramental form of the bread and wine, or merely present in some cryptic manner as might perhaps be interpreted from the designation 'mystical body of Christ'. The formal Church reaction on this occasion was forthright, and to stress that the Eucharist was the *real* body of Christ, the original adjective 'mystical' was dropped in order to avoid any misunderstanding. In time, the word reappeared but as an attachment to the description of the Church, which as an organisation began to be referred to increasingly as the mystical body of Christ.

The question for us today is whether this reversal in terminology

---

[15] ibid., p. 92.
[16] Referred to by McPartlan, *Sacrament of Salvation,* p. 30.

is a cause for concern. I believe the answer is 'yes', and in my view this is well expressed by Paul McPartlan:

> Whereas the thoughts of the Fathers of the Church tended to flow naturally and smoothly from Christ through the Eucharist to the Church (the *corpus verum*), now the train of thought tended to stop short at the presence of Christ in the Eucharist itself and the link between the Eucharist and the Church began to be neglected. What was now greatly studied was simply the way in which Christ was present in the Eucharist under the forms of bread and wine.[17]

The Scholastic theologians of the thirteenth century began to use the idea of 'transubstantiation', meaning that the substance of the bread and wine was transformed into the substance of the body and blood of Christ in *truth* – not just as an *image* or an *appearance* or a *figure*, and this became official Catholic teaching at the Fourth Lateran Council (1215). Shortly after this, at the Council of Lyons II in 1274, the Eucharist became listed as just one of seven sacraments of the Church.

I am not disputing the validity of the doctrine of transubstantiation, or implying that it represents a departure from the understanding of the early Church Fathers. They would have had no difficulty accepting this later formulation, but may perhaps have wondered why so much attention was devoted to producing such an explanation. In the words of Henri deLubac, what began as 'the mystery to understand' became 'the miracle to believe' and one of the consequences was that, confronted by such a miracle, people felt unworthy to receive the consecrated bread.[18] To attend Mass and receive Holy Communion was no longer an automatic practice and the Fourth Lateran Council considered it necessary to decree that the faithful should partake of the sacrament at least

---

[17] McPartlan, *Eucharist: The Body of Christ*, p. 49.
[18] Referred to by McPartlan, *Sacrament of Salvation*, p. 38.

once a year at Easter, i.e. the origin of what became known as 'Easter duties'.

The real consequence of this change of wording and emphasis was that the Eucharist was no longer seen as the 'encompassing orbit and dynamic centre of ecclesial existence'. It had simply become one of several actions which formed part of the Church's armoury. The Church had, in a sense, become a juridical institution in its own right, a body which was administered by bishops and run on a day-to-day basis by priests.[19] DeLubac's concept that 'the Eucharist makes the Church' had changed into the notion that 'the Church makes the Eucharist'.

The Council of Trent (1545–63)

The Council was called to reaffirm Catholic teaching in response to the sixteenth-century Protestant Reformation in Europe and produced two decrees on the Eucharist. One focused on its sacramental nature (concerned primarily with transubstantiation) and the other dealt with the Mass as a sacrifice. The former confirmed the *real presence* of Christ in the Eucharist, not simply as a presence in the elements of bread and wine but involving a real change in the substance of these elements.

The second decree was to counter the proposition that the Mass was merely a commemoration of Christ's sacrifice as an historic event. His death and resurrection were acknowledged as a once-and-for-all occurrence, but one which of its nature is nevertheless 'engraved in the heavens and over-arches history', such that it can be present and indeed *is* present in our midst in all its redeeming power at every Mass.[20]

These decrees set the parameters of Catholic teaching on the Eucharist, namely, that a 'real change' occurs in the substance of the bread and wine and that the sacrifice of Jesus is 'made real'

---

[19] McPartlan, *Eucharist: The Body of Christ*, p. 52.
[20] ibid., p. 57.

at each Mass. While the assertiveness of the Council's teaching is evident, one of the criticisms of Trent might be that it failed to properly connect these two decrees. In other words, it provided the means to answer questions that might be raised, but without presenting a comprehensive and readily understandable overview of the Eucharist in the context of the Church.

In the aftermath of the Council, in 1570, Pope Pius V produced a missal for the Mass which contained an express papal prohibition against any change. This was the state in which eucharistic doctrine and practice was to remain for almost the next 400 years, until Vatican II and a new missal authorised by Pope Paul VI.

Vatican II (1962–65)

The Council's 'Constitution on the Sacred Liturgy' (*Sacrosanctum Concilium*) described every liturgical celebration as an action of Christ the priest and his body the Church and thereby a pre-eminently sacred action (*SC #7*). The liturgy was seen to comprise unchangeable elements which were divinely instituted and other elements which could, and indeed should, be subject to change if they suffered from the intrusion of anything which was out of harmony with their inner nature or which inhibited the full and active participation of the whole Christian community (*SC #21*).

The Mass is singled out as being entrusted to the Church to perpetuate the sacrifice of Jesus on the cross throughout the ages until he returns, a memorial of his death and resurrection, a sacrament of love, a sign of unity and bond of charity, 'a paschal banquet in which Christ is received, the mind is filled with grace and a pledge of future glory is given to us' (*SC #47*). The Eucharist is properly understood therefore as a *sacramental sacrifice*, in which we truly receive the body of Christ and become the body of Christ participating in communion with one another in his own sacrifice and self-gift to his Father.

Each Mass is understood as a collective participation in the *live* memorial of the once-and-for-all death and resurrection of

Jesus, at the same time anticipating our future life in heaven, 'towards which we journey as pilgrims' (*SC* #8). Against this background, the Council ordered that the rite of the Mass should be revised in such a way that the intrinsic nature and purpose of its several parts, as well as the connection between them, might more clearly be shown to achieve devout and active participation by the faithful (*SC* #50).

This overall aim was seen as a two-part exercise. First, to simplify the rite by omitting duplications and reinstating other elements which had been lost over the years, but always keeping the ancient tradition of the Fathers of the Church as the appropriate guide (*SC* #50). Second, those holding pastoral responsibility in the Church were charged not merely to ensure that the laws governing valid and lawful celebrations of the liturgy were observed, but to ensure also that the faithful take part in the liturgy fully aware of what they are doing, actively engaged in the rite and enriched by it (*SC* #11).

The Council further emphasised that liturgical services and the Mass in particular were not private functions, but the celebration of the whole body which is the Church, the 'sacrament of unity', the holy people, united and organised under their bishops (*SC* #26). The temperament and tradition of the different peoples who make up the Church were also acknowledged and, subject to the prior approval of the Apostolic See, these qualities and talents were to be cultivated and fostered in seeking to admit anything in people's way of life not indissolubly bound up with superstition and error and which can be harmonised with the true and authentic spirit of the liturgy (SC #37).

As mentioned previously, there is a common perception that Vatican II replaced Latin with the vernacular, but in reality this is simply not the case. The continued use of Latin was, however, subject to relaxations in accord with approved regulations relating to specific territorial ecclesiastic authority where the vernacular was considered to be of advantage to people in readings, directives and in some prayers and chants (*SC* #36). In practice, the vernacular became the norm for most ecclesiastical authorities within a comparatively short period, albeit that Rome reserved the right to approve all translations from the original Latin.

The Mass today

The inevitable question is this: How successful has Vatican II been in achieving its twin objectives of adapting the liturgy to the needs of our age and enriching the faithful by improving their awareness and participation (see *SC* #1, 11)? In my view, the results to date are less than satisfactory on both counts and I offer the following observations.

(i) The use of the vernacular must constitute a definite gain by enabling all the faithful to understand and participate in the prayers of the Mass. I find it difficult to imagine how or why the public prayer of the Church could ever be other than in the language of those participating.

This said, the choice of vocabulary is dictated entirely by Rome, with one 'authorised version' of the Mass for all English-speaking peoples worldwide. This is despite the Council's undertaking to avoid rigid uniformity in the liturgy (see above, *SC* #37), and at the time of writing we are awaiting the introduction of a new authorised version. The claim for this latest text is that it more accurately reflects the original Latin, which makes one wonder why we were given a less accurate translation in the first place. Also, with regard to the development of the liturgy, why is Latin regarded as the original and sole language base to apply in perpetuity?

Unlike Latin, English is a living language. Its grammar, syntax, individual nuances and idiomatic applications are in a continuous state of development. Moreover, the results of this process are far from uniform across English-speaking peoples, as visits to the US, Australia, South Africa, etc. will attest. And yet English is treated by Rome as if it was a single indigenous language, on which it imposes one 'common' text which takes no account of either ongoing development or country-by-country variations in usage.

The result, in my opinion, can at best be described as 'bland' and enforcing such a policy represents an impoverishment of the language's full potential to inspire and enthuse.

(ii) The importance of Scripture was emphasised by Vatican II (*SC #24*) and accompanied by a call to provide more varied and suitable readings (*SC #35[1]*). As a result, each Sunday Mass now includes four readings from the Bible, two from the Old Testament and two from the New Testament, and these are followed by a homily which is intended to explain the choice of readings, their interconnectedness and the collective message they convey. However, with the 'collect' of the day, the Credo and the bidding prayers, the congregation will have been exposed to eight separate items of information in the first 25–30 minutes of the Mass, during which time they will have been required to stand three times and sit down twice. Is this too ambitious an agenda to be effective?

To cite myself as an example, it is easy to switch off and remain so from the first reading if it is not properly introduced in the context of that Sunday's sequence of readings, or if, as is sometimes the case, it does not strike an immediate chord of relevance. This is more an issue of presentation rather than content, but in order to generate the 'warm and lively appreciation of Sacred Scripture' which was encouraged by Vatican II (*SC #24*), I consider that greater attention needs to be devoted to this area.

For a majority of the faithful, there is possibly only one weekly encounter with Scripture, which is at Mass on Sunday. In my view, retelling the story of God's communication with us calls for a more expansive 'in the round' approach rather than simply delivering four set readings and expecting a short homily to adequately explain why they have been chosen together and their underlying message.

(iii) The introduction of new eucharistic prayers is a further benefit resulting from Vatican II. With the third Eucharistic Prayer in particular, the specific invocation of the Spirit (*epiclesis*), asking the Holy Spirit to descend and dwell within the bread and wine and in the congregation, points us back to our common heritage with the Church in the East where this aspect has always remained a prominent element of the liturgy..

It is evident that significant historical and biblical scholarship has gone into these latest compositions, but how widely is this appreciated within the Church? What is the general level of awareness of how the particular form and content of these prayers came about? I cannot ever recollect hearing a proper explanation during the course of a Sunday Mass, which in my view is a further example of impoverishment as well as being a lost opportunity for what could be a productive series of homilies.

(iv) My real concern is the way in which people may perceive the Mass as an event. What is it we believe we are attending and why do we continue to do so? The readings, if listened to and with some proper explanation, can be seen as conveying a message or an instruction, but what about the remainder – the offertory, the consecration, the sign of peace, the reception of Holy Communion? What is taking place here and what does our individual and collective participation amount to?

For many of us, Sunday Mass is a predictable routine of readings and ceremony, and regular attendance can lead to fluctuating levels of attentive concentration – like driving a car along a customary route and returning home almost oblivious to what occurred around you during that particular journey. For some people, attendance at Mass may be purely a matter of habit, or prompted by the fear or threat of mortal sin for not doing so, which are hardly the best of motives – but at least a physical presence does offer an opportunity for an explanation in order to improve their appreciation of what is taking place and why.

So what is the awareness or appreciation that could otherwise be lacking? First, I consider that the institution of the Mass needs to be viewed as an inherent part of God's original and continuing plan of self-communication with humankind, rather than just a single event in history. In this way it becomes possible to recognise more clearly the richness and continuity of our biblical heritage, the immanence of the Holy Spirit in our daily lives, and our place and purpose in God's unfolding plan.

Second, the Mass can sometimes appear to be a series of individual parts which, although collectively pointing towards Jesus, do not always convey the dynamism or the sense of his continuing involvement which he intended when instigating the Eucharist. At the Last Supper, Jesus offered himself to his Father and also to his disciples in the form of bread and wine. By participating in this meal the disciples effectively became his body and they too formed part of his offering to his Father. Here, then, is a perfect act of atonement, i.e. *at-one-ment* with God: a body to be sacrificed, a body to be raised in glory, a body which for all time and in every place will continue to re-enact and make present the essence of this sacrifice.

The significant words here are 'continue to make present', meaning that every Mass is intended to be a 'live' event that unites each one of us to Jesus and to one another as fellow participants in the whole episode of our redemption. We actively participate in Jesus' death and resurrection and the descent of the Holy Spirit – Good Friday, Easter Sunday and Pentecost all in one. Referring to the Council of Trent, the *Catechism* records that because Jesus' priesthood was not to end with his death, he wanted to leave his body, the Church, a visible sacrifice by which the once-for-all bloody sacrifice on the cross would be re-presented (made present) until the end of the world and its salutary power be applied to the forgiveness of the sins we daily commit (#1366).

In my view, it is difficult to imagine a better motivation to attend Mass than an awareness of the magnitude of the event in which we are called to participate and make real on each and every occasion. In practice, I consider that the form of our present liturgy falls well short of conveying this same heightened sense of continually re-presenting the life and eventual sacrifice of Jesus and can often appear more in the nature of a weekly testimonial relating to a past event. We simply recall that at a particular point in time, Jesus instigated a celebratory meal, went on to suffer and die on our behalf, rose again, having put things right, and has long since been back in heaven at God's right hand.

At the consecration, Catholic belief is that the bread and wine are changed into the body and blood of Jesus. This is firmly based on biblical testimony and the tradition of the Church through the centuries. As St John Chrysostom (d. AD 407) declared, 'It is not man that causes the things offered to become the Body and Blood of Christ, but he who was crucified for us, Christ himself.' And in order to explain the change, St Ambrose (d. AD 397) held that if Christ's word could make from nothing what did not exist, why could it not change existing things into what they were not before on the grounds that 'it is no less a feat to give things their original nature than to change their nature'.[21]

Centuries later, it was considered necessary to seek to formalise the process by which this change or conversion took place and attention was directed towards the interplay between the 'accidents' or the appearances of an item (i.e., what the senses can grasp) and its 'substance', namely, its ultimate reality. At the consecration, therefore, the appearance of the bread and wine is stated to remain as before, but their reality or substance is changed by the power of the Holy Spirit into that of the body and blood of Christ. This is the doctrine of transubstantiation.

I have no difficulty with this formally declared teaching of the Church, but I believe it needs to be presented and understood in the broader context of the *sacramental sacrifice* of Jesus and the way in which it continues directly to touch and involve each of us. To reiterate the thoughts of Henri deLubac, our focus should remain on the overall mystery in which we are participants rather than trying to treat an object of faith as an object of science that is seen as a system of truths and precepts imposing themselves only on the basis of a certain number of facts.[22]

In other words, the acceptance of the Eucharist as what we

---

[21] See *Catechism* #1375.
[22] Referred to by Komonchak, *Theology and Culture at Mid-Century*, p. 582.

claim it to be has to reside within the realm of faith and trust, as acknowledged by the *Catechism* when it states that the change in the bread and wine occurs in a way which surpasses our understanding (#1333). To claim otherwise could run the risk of specific words and actions of the Mass becoming treated as intrinsic to the process, a precise or magical formula to produce the 'miracle to be believed', and where any minor deviation might therefore render the whole invalid. This was certainly not how the Eucharist was understood by the Fathers of the Church, and nor should it be by us.

I began this chapter by expressing my surprise at hearing a public announcement for a Catholic Mass and I am prompted to close on a similar note. My surprise on this second occasion is that despite the eloquent rhetoric which has been applied to the Eucharist from Vatican II onwards, our pastoral leadership seems to me to have made such little progress in promoting the liturgically educated and enthused eucharistic communities hoped for by the Council.

The Eucharist has been analysed, synthesised, packaged and dispensed over the years, but without necessarily conveying its full import as the active centre and essential focus of our Christian life. For many people it may continue to be thought of principally as an encounter with a regular church ritual which is deemed mandatory on Sundays and holy days.

A more expansive and certainly more inspirational description is provided by Paul McPartlan:

> Overall, we may imagine local churches celebrating the Eucharist around their bishop, being woven together in a vast tapestry through time and across space by ties of apostolic succession and collegiality, respectively, which simply express the profound reality that, whenever the Eucharist is celebrated, in any place at any time, only one heavenly mystery is present and one great purpose is at work; the one Christ is gathering the scattered children of God into the one Church ... that

these countless celebrations are not ultimately many but one. The integrity of the Church's witness to the Gospel demands that the oneness be evident.[23]

---

[23] McPartlan, *Sacrament of Salvation*, p. 67.

Part Three

Where Do We Go From Here?

9

Taking Stock

The Catholic Church is the largest and longest-serving institution in the world. It has survived external persecutions, internal dissents and the challenge over the centuries of needing to respond to social and political change. Today it functions as a sovereign state, has a network of over 3,000 dioceses in virtually every country, a pastoral leadership of more than 4,000 bishops and a membership which comprises some 17% of the world's population. It is an impressive record when one considers that the entire Church was accommodated in one upper room at its inauguration on the first Christian celebration of Pentecost.

In terms of purpose, the Church's goal is to establish the kingdom of God throughout the world, not in a geographical sense but as an activity which takes place in people's hearts based on the values of justice and love. The life and teachings of Jesus form the essential ingredient in its outlook and approach and while the fullness of the kingdom or the reign of God may not be experienced in this life, the Church continues to be a means towards this end, a sign that always points towards it.

The real measure of success is therefore our effectiveness in responding to this task, for which we can offer positive evidence. At the same time I suspect that an external performance assessment might include observations such as 'could have done better ... can easily become distracted ... finds it difficult to admit to mistakes ... can sometimes be highly judgemental ... sometimes unsympathetic ... is often slow to implement initiatives'. All of these are human foibles and a reminder perhaps that God's self-communication is not a one-way exercise and has to rely on a human response and input, however inadequate this may be.

The background to the Bible has always been the word of God given expression by the words and experiences of the authors, a divinely inspired compass for a journey rather than a divinely dictated end product. Our mandate from Jesus did not include a detailed operational manual, but came with the promise of ongoing support from his Spirit. It is for us to work with the Spirit in order to develop and expand our understanding of Jesus' message and to find ways in which this might best be expressed to meet the needs of successive generations.

Yet we sometimes seem to act as if we already hold the full definitive text of God's plan for creation, together with answers to all conceivable questions for which total conformity and obedience are demanded. As this is described by Michael Morwood, we have fully worked out and put into neat theological categories all there is to ever know about God and all future questions and issues can be dealt with within these categories. God's surprises are finished.[1]

Clearly we need to hold fast to our divinely inspired beliefs, but this does not and should not preclude us, with God's help, from continuing to seek to improve our understanding and appreciation of their true import. We have a responsibility to avail ourselves of all the benefits of modern scholarship in order to be as certain as we can be at any one time in our interpretation of all that we proclaim.

This set the brief for Vatican II and as a result of their deliberations, the Council Fathers highlighted a need for change in a number of areas. They did not produce immediate solutions for every situation and it is evident from many of the texts that it was found necessary to reach compromises, but they did set a

---

[1] Morwood, *Tomorrow's Catholic*, p. 130.

new direction for the Church's pastoral response. If we are to keep alive the wish of Pope John XXIII and the formally expressed aim of the Council to be attuned to the signs of the times, we need to continue to build on the insights of Vatican II with the benefit of our ongoing experiences.

Unfortunately, I sense that our current pastoral leadership is resolved to move in precisely the opposite direction: to draw a line under what is now a 40-year-old event and pursue a policy of 'conserve and preserve'; to treat what is currently being said and done as unquestionably correct and to apply the Church's institutional influence and power to stifle open discussion through an appeal to notions of loyalty.

In previous chapters I have made reference to various events from history which in my view have contributed to the way in which we presently see ourselves and function as 'the Church'. These seem to me to fall under three broad headings.

Copyright

I believe we may have convinced ourselves over the years that we hold the patent on God and full performance rights for Jesus. In the Western Church in particular, as Geoffrey Robinson puts it, there has been a passion to analyse God, to set out lists of his attributes, to attempt to penetrate the mystery of the Trinity and in general to fill books with our human comments about him.[2]

As a result, we sometimes presume to talk about God in the same way as we refer to other people and things, whereas at best we are only able to use images and thoughts that grasp at insights. Our language and intellect are unable to bridge the gap between the finite us and the infinite transcendence that must be God in order for God to be God and not just some larger-than-life human

---

[2] Robinson, *Confronting Power and Sex in the Catholic Church*, p. 28.

equivalent. To repeat yet again the wise caution of St Thomas Aquinas, we know *that* God is, not *what* God is, other than by his actions, and even here we should not try to confine God's works to what our present knowledge horizons enable us to qualify and quantify.

We claim that Jesus was a person like us in all things except sin and even with this caveat, he has become an even more tempting target for us to claim exclusive ownership. We have the Gospel accounts of his life to include the commissioning of St Peter and the other disciples, and it is only a short step from this to formulate the view that, as his appointed successor, the Church has inherited the same divine pedigree for all that we may say and do subsequently.

By way of examples, in order to support the teaching on original sin, the 1994 *Catechism* makes the claim by reference to a Pauline text that the Church 'has the mind of Christ' (#389). What is meant by this? And later there is the statement to the effect that God wants everyone to be a Catholic because this is his Son's Church, 'where humanity must rediscover its unity and salvation. The Church is the world reconciled' (#845).

An exaggerated opinion of our divine inheritance can run the risk of our coming to regard the Church as a 'third source' of our knowledge of God alongside the Bible and the evidence of the world around and within us. This is highlighted by Geoffrey Robinson, who says that in the context of God's eternal plan, the Church is meant to be a means by which this becomes a reality in the world, a sign of its presence, but it is not the only means and it can never be more than a sign; it can never be the total embodiment of the eternal plan.[3]

In other words, we need to avoid becoming introspective, treating ourselves as the goal of our own strivings, assuming we already have all the answers, and seeing our principal objective as preserving particular ritual or worship systems rather than these

---

[3] ibid., p. 78.

supporting us in our primary purpose of extending Jesus' offer of life to the world at large. Our Christian faith is first and foremost faith in a person and the story of his life, death and resurrection, and it is from this that other truths and behavioural indicators can flow.

In Robinson's view, without this personal relationship, the truths will become lifeless, the norms of living will be burdensome tasks and the worship will be empty. With the relationship, the truths will come alive, the norms of living will be the most natural things in the world and the worship will be life-giving. Take the personal relationship out of religion, and all that is left is an empty formalism.[4]

Ministry

We profess a common fellowship in Jesus through baptism, but we have allowed the Church to develop into a distinctly two-tier organisation that comprises the 'ordained' and the 'non-ordained'.

The former account for under 1% of the total, but through numerous tiers of authority exercise unquestioning control over all facets of theology and liturgy, together with Church administration, finance and governance. The ordained manage and allocate their own people resources as they consider appropriate and operate a self-administered internal process for succession which is conducted for the most part with no outside participation and little overall accountability.

At the personal level, we have tended to create a mystique relating to the office of priest, implying that in some way a priest is 'taken up' to a separate and higher level. The letter to the Hebrews (5:1) is frequently cited in support of this, with the result that the sacred becomes assigned to clerics and identified

---

[4] ibid., p. 41.

with the actions that are reserved to them and the secular pertains to the laity or actions forbidden to clerics.

As Geoffrey Robinson observes, if Catholics are to integrate their faith into their lives, a dualism between the sacred and the secular needs to be avoided, as without exception we all live in the world and it is a world that is both sacred and secular. This was recognised by Pope Paul VI when he spoke of the whole Church having an authentic secular dimension, and it is because of this that we are able to fulfil our role of offering life to the full to the whole cosmos.[5]

A comparatively recent example of clerical 'separateness' seems to have emerged within our eucharistic prayers. The First Eucharistic Prayer (the original Roman Canon), which was the sole authorised version prior to Vatican II, includes a prayer for the Pope and the Diocesan Bishop as the focus of unity for the universal and the local Church and this is followed by a prayer for 'all who hold and teach the Catholic faith that comes to us from the apostles'. However, in the principal new versions (Eucharistic Prayers II–IV), there is now a call for prayers for the clergy who are treated as a separate category distinct from the rest of the faithful, and in the Second Eucharistic Prayer there is no mention at all of anyone else at this point in the prayer.

So in terms of a priestly ministry, where can we look to identify what Jesus may have intended? The Gospels record that he called together a group of people from amongst his disciples to be the principal witnesses of all that he was to say and do. These were the Twelve, whom Jesus introduced to the Eucharist as his continuing memorial and from whom we can reasonably assume that he expected some process for succession. Beyond this, however, we need to avoid reaching too specific a conclusion on who and what this might entail.

For example, the Gospels of St Matthew and St Mark move

---

[5] Referred to in ibid., p. 296.

easily from references to the Twelve to mentions of apostles and/or disciples generally, making it difficult on occasion to know whom the writer is describing and which function belongs to whom. St Matthew records the solemn promise made to St Peter that whatever he should bind or loose on earth would be endorsed in heaven (Matthew 16:17–19), and yet two verses later this same promise is made to 'the disciples' (Matthew 18:18), which I take to support the view that Jesus purposely intended the whole Church to have some share in his authority.

In terms of succession, we read in Acts of a meeting to select a replacement for Judas, which was led by St Peter on behalf of the remaining eleven, together with 'about a hundred and twenty persons in the congregation'. Following a period of prayer, all those who were present drew lots to select Matthias (Acts 1:15–26). The next chapter describes the feast of Pentecost, when we are told they were all present in the upper room and experienced the presence of the Spirit (Acts 2:1–4). This is effectively the inauguration ceremony of the Church, but who does 'they' refer to? Is it restricted to the remaining eleven, or does it indicate a wider congregation of the size and composition that elected Matthias, or perhaps the group which included Mary, the mother of Jesus, and who are recorded as frequently joining the apostles in prayer (Acts 1:12–14)?

The conclusion which I consider it reasonable to reach from these and other related narratives from the New Testament is that Jesus purposely singled out an original group of twelve, who with Peter as lead spokesman would in some way form the basis for the community of believers. He had indicated the form of ministry he was seeking, namely, one of service and persuasion rather than dominance and coercion, but thereafter it would be for them to decide how best to develop and expand a pastoral ministry, and to determine individual and collective roles in concert with the members of the communities they were to serve.

It is evident also that the Twelve and their immediate successors, together with the presbyters who were originally elected to lead individual domestic assemblies, continued to follow the pattern set by Jesus of not claiming or presuming a priestly status in the manner of the Jewish tradition. This began to change in later centuries with the introduction of the whole 'sacred apparatus' pertaining to the ministry of the Eucharist and resulted in the common priesthood of the people of God (originally *laos*, 'people', without distinction) becoming divided into clergy and laity.

As this is described by Michael Richards:

> The clergy/laity distinction is a cultural not a theological one; it is foreign to the New Testament and has masked the inner unity of the Church. Properly speaking, to be 'of the Church' is to be 'lay': someone dedicated to the gathering together of the People of God.
>
> To promote the work of the Church in the world as the joint task of all members, one must remember that in the people of God there is a single class and that in that context all are priests of God, all worshipping him according to the manner in which they respond to their individual vocation in the world.[6]

Ministry in the Church today has become virtually synonymous with an all-male ordained priesthood. The present form and structure of this priesthood is stated, or at least implied, by our pastoral leadership to mirror a divine blueprint which was issued by Jesus and so cannot be open to change. Further debate is discouraged and discussions on matters such as married priests and women priests are formally prohibited in official circles. The allocation of duties in the mission of the Church looks, therefore, to be fixed in perpetuity.

From a purely practical standpoint, this present attitude and approach can only impact adversely on the workings of the Church as the overall number of active ordained continues to decline.

---

[6] Michael Richards, *A People of Priests* (Darton, Longman and Todd, 1995), p. 61.

This has been an acute problem for many years in some parts of the world, but many traditional Catholic countries which were previously 'net exporters' of priests are themselves being forced to amalgamate and even close parishes domestically. One is forced to conclude that the ongoing sacramental life of the Church must therefore be considered less important than maintaining historic regulations which pertain to the style and state of life of those charged with its delivery.

In addition, an authoritative ministry with little evidence of consultation and/or accountability is unlikely in my view to generate wholehearted support in today's milieu. The frequent retort, of course, is that the Church is not a democracy, which in respect of our underlying deposit of faith I would certainly agree with, but must this be assumed to preclude seeking a wider consensus for how this might best be understood, presented and delivered? Advances in technology now enable 'Rome' to oversee and exercise total and immediate control over virtually every aspect of Church life, but not, it would seem, also to listen to the views of the Church at large in the long-standing tradition of the *sensus fidei*.[7]

I believe there is a noticeable sense of disillusionment and frustration within the Church that a 'ruling clerical caste' operates in accordance with its own agenda and is becoming increasingly remote from people's day-to-day lives in terms of their outlook and concerns. This is causing many people, and especially the young, to look elsewhere for the answers and support they are seeking.

Happiness

This may seem a strange choice of heading, but I believe it is a relevant factor when considering how we ought to set about

---

[7] See Robinson, *Confronting Power and Sex in the Catholic Church*, p. 146.

responding to the message of Jesus. The practice of religion is all too often perceived as calling for a self- imposed and perpetual state of personal austerity. For some people it can even be expressed as obedience out of a sense of fear.

The *Penny Catechism* states that we have been created to know God, love God and serve God in this world and be happy with him for ever in the next (#2). We are also urged to remain on constant guard against the three enemies of our soul, namely, the devil, the world and the flesh (#348). Taken together, these might suggest that happiness is really meant as a reward in the future for duties we are required to perform in the present and that we should be suspicious of any happiness we derive now from earthly activities.

Yet happiness is a God-given emotion which should connect us rather than isolate us from day-to-day life. It is through our emotions that we experience the world around us and come to see it as a source of revelation – the beauty and grandeur of our physical environment, the uniqueness of our individual presence, the love and fulfilment in personal relationships, the joys of giving and receiving, and so on.

These experiences are surely a foretaste of what we believe is in store for us when we reach the fullness of God, not a competing agenda. As followers of the promise of Jesus, we should be the world's complete and unashamed optimists in all that we say and do and in the enthusiasm with which we engage with other people and life in general. To repeat the words of St Irenaeus, 'The glory of God is the human person fully alive.'

We seem instead to have allowed the example of Jesus' life that so inspired and enthused his early followers to become submerged within a wholly codified theology and set of practices which simply call for intellectual assent and conformity. It is a response which is, so to speak, directed more towards a compliance with the small print of the travel regulations rather than encouraging a sense of adventure for the journey itself.

In my view, one of the factors which continues to shape the

Catholic outlook on life is our inherited attitude towards sin. We are told that we are born with it and need to be cleansed, we are constantly exposed to it and need to be protected, we regularly succumb to it and require reconciliation. We are asked to acknowledge our sinfulness at the beginning of every Mass before we are able to begin the readings.

I am not doubting the existence of sin or evil, merely questioning what appears on occasions to be an excessive preoccupation. As human beings we are born into a world of bacteria which continues to surround us on a daily basis and from time to time we may fall prey to its effects, but if we are continuously stressing our vulnerability and its potential consequences we would surely all be raging hypochondriacs. In a religious context I believe this is what many Catholics are prone to be, which in some cases has produced an enduring sense of personal guilt.

We are the 'Easter People'.[8] We profess a belief in the risen Lord who broke the chains of sin and who told us that he had come so that we would have life to the full (John 10:10). We need to believe Jesus, not just claim to believe *in* Jesus. Life is for living, sensibly and sensitively towards others, but not continuously looking over our shoulder for potential theological health hazards. I believe there is much wisdom in the words of the Jewish writer who said that 'people will be called to account by God for all the legitimate pleasures they failed to enjoy'.[9]

I believe that we, as the Church, could be open to the same underlying indictment as that which might be levelled against Adam and Eve – namely, of imagining ourselves capable of becoming equivalent to God on earth; of judging that we are able to reach decisions purely because of who we are rather than because of what we have been asked to do.

We were invited by Jesus to follow his message and example,

---

[8] The title of a report produced by the Bishops of England and Wales, following the National Synod held in Liverpool in 1980.
[9] Referred to by Robinson, *Confronting Power and Sex in the Catholic Church*, p. 36.

which came with the assurance that he would always remain our point of reference. We have been associated with this task for almost 2,000 years, but seem to act on occasions as if we no longer consider that we need a point of reference. To repeat the earlier statement from the *Catechism*, 'we have the mind of Christ', and may imagine from this that we also possess all the answers, that we are the 'perfect society', the complete repository of truth.

As a result, our unity in faith as the people of God can easily become confused with ecclesial uniformity and conformity, where any question is automatically treated as an act of dissent. We find it difficult as an institution to admit to mistakes or readily countenance change, in case this might be taken to imply that we could have been wrong the first time around. All this runs contrary to the practice of the early Church, when decisions were often superseded through a process of thought and prayer, giving way to more scholarly prudence, or if something which was hidden became known.[10]

Vatican II reaffirmed the inalienable principle of Christian freedom in several documents. It is most clearly enunciated in the 'Decree on Ecumenism' (*Unitatis Redintegratio*): 'Whilst preserving unity in essentials, let all in the Church according to the office entrusted to them preserve a proper freedom in the various forms of spiritual life and discipline, in the variety of liturgical rites and even in the theological elaborations of revealed truth. In all things let charity prevail' (*UR* #4).

Freedom is described by the canonist James Coriden as a 'polestar' for the Church, with the ministry of the canon lawyer being to ensure that the Church remains a 'protected zone of freedom', one that is free from domination, despotism, coercion, intimidation and control that stifles the Spirit.[11] The corollary, of course, is that our gift of freedom has to be open to the possibility

---

[10] ibid., p. 241.
[11] James Coriden, *Canon Law as Ministry* (Paulist Press, 2000), p. 79.

of making mistakes, but I judge this to be God's way of enabling us to grow, by having to continue to search for truth and take responsibility for all that we believe and do in this struggle.

As this is described by Gabriel Daley, God's truth is not handed over as an easy grace and, while open theological enquiry can be a hazardous business which gives rise to tensions and factions, it is how ancient truths are kept in intellectual working order. Moreover, in Daley's considered opinion, most of the conflicts which may arise in the process of faith's self-understanding are not between straight affirmation or straight denial, but about meaning, about making sense of what we profess to believe – about interpretation.[12]

The doctrine of papal infallibility is our ultimate assurance in this regard, but we need to remain on guard to ensure that, by design or otherwise, it does not become attached subliminally to each Church statement and create the erroneous impression that every official pronouncement must carry the same 'divine imprimatur' of authenticity. A more balanced summation of the doctrine in my view is provided by Hans Kung:

> The promise of Jesus Christ was not that the Church will never make mistakes but that it will survive its mistakes, for the truth of Jesus Christ will always be present in the Church – tarnished and even obscured, but always there to be rediscovered. The promise is that in spite of many errors in detail, the Church will be maintained in the basic truth of the Great Tradition [the continuing process of handing on from generation to generation], and that the ugliness in the Church will never completely destroy its underlying beauty. The Church's faith will often be weak, its love lukewarm, its hope wavering, but that on what its faith is based, its love rooted and its hope is built will always endure.[13]

---

[12] Daley, 'Faith and Theology', *The Tablet*, 18–25 April 1981, p. 446.
[13] Referred to by Robinson, *Confronting Power and Sex in the Catholic Church*, p. 260.

10

Writing the Next Chapter

It is Jesus Christ alone we must present to the world. Outside this we have no reason to exist.[1]

This was the view expressed by Pope John Paul I on the last day of his life in September 1978. One might wonder where this could have led him, and indeed us, if his papacy had not been so tragically short.

As it is, the Pope's words are unlikely to come as a surprise. After all, we operate under the name 'Christian', we listen to the words of Jesus in our Sunday readings and we try to give example to them in the way we behave. We are members of an organisation that is dedicated to perpetuating his memory and we have a highly developed and elaborate support apparatus to assist us in the process.

My concern, however, is that we may have become more focused on the apparatus than the message it is intended to serve, and may identify with the practices of the faith more closely than with the beliefs themselves. My generation in particular was taught by rote and to some extent we have perhaps continued ever since out of habit to follow a given set of precepts and comply with stated rules of membership. But is this a living and developing faith?

---

[1] Referred to by Gerald O'Collins, *Jesus, A Portrait* (Darton, Longman and Todd, 2008), p. vii.

In his book *Tomorrow's Catholic*, Michael Morwood highlights the distinction between what he describes as our 'foundational belief' concerning God, Jesus and ourselves and the various means which are at our disposal to help animate and sustain this belief. Our foundational belief comprises the following.

1. God is everywhere, loving and to be trusted absolutely.
2. Jesus is divine and human and his way of living and loving shows us our potential as well as our destiny as human beings.
3. We are sharers of the same Spirit of God that moved in Jesus. We are the body of Christ.

In terms of the means for keeping this in focus, we have stories (sacraments), teaching (doctrine), authority (laws), liturgy (prayer forms) and devotions (customs). These features of church experience should continuously point us towards our foundational belief and this is the criterion by which we evaluate their effectiveness for purpose.[2]

Thus in Jesus we become aware of our relatedness to God, who is not remote or demanding, who does not require us to win his favour as he already has unshakeable fatherly love for all of us. Jesus himself is both divine and human and therefore what we are if we take our inherent potential to its fullest possible level. Our awareness of this, and our call to be the body of Christ with him as our head, is the offer of life that we are able to present to the world.

In Morwood's view, we need to question seriously any stories that make us fearful of God, that lead us to imagine that he is distant or that we have to earn his mercy. If teaching or preaching suggests in any way that Jesus is not really as human as the rest of us, it would represent a shift in our foundational belief. And if what we believe about real presence in the consecrated bread

[2] Morwood, *Tomorrow's Catholic*, p. 115.

and speculation on how that happens becomes more important than our belief that we are the real presence of the Spirit of God in the world, we would be losing focus on a fundamental truth about ourselves.[3]

At the same time, it is important for us to retain safeguards which, in the words of Geoffrey Robinson, prevent the idea emerging of a god of soft and indulgent love, a god so apparently loving that nothing is asked of people and they are challenged to nothing.[4] Our current social environment with its emphasis on relativism and political correctness is particularly conducive to such a notion, where the followers of this god can go so far as to deny the existence of right and wrong, personal responsibility or standards of conduct.

The challenge for us in the Church today is to maintain the right balance, to prevent our foundational faith becoming subsumed by excess qualifications and conditions or watered down by misguided concepts. Vatican II saw the benefit of revisiting the Church's long and rich tradition to look for help in this regard. The Council did its job, but in my view we still have some way to go with our own job of assimilating and applying its findings.

We seem to have allowed the distinction between faith and practice to become blurred. We are so immersed in 'due process' that its preservation and protection, to include those who are associated with it, can easily become a primary consideration, as is sadly evidenced in many of the recent reports concerning child abuse incidents. There appears also to be a presumption in some quarters that the faithful can always be relied upon to follow, and if directed towards a return to 'Catholic practices' as they were before Vatican II, that will solve all our present problems. It will not.

In my opinion, we need to return to first principles. We need to improve the level of awareness of what our relatedness to God

---

[3] ibid., p. 117.
[4] Robinson, *Confronting Power and Sex in the Catholic Church*, p. 27.

really does mean. We must better appreciate the concept of God's presence in the whole of creation and in us in particular who have been created in his image and likeness. It is vital that we take fully on board what this description means for us as individuals living in relationships as human beings. This is very much a family affair, in that we are all, without exception, children of the same loving Father and we have the promise of this from Jesus, our 'elder brother', who in the fullness of time will return us intact as a family to our place of origin in God.

In the meantime, we might usefully make a start by ridding ourselves of the harm dualism has caused in Christian thought and attitudes, of setting one over the other – soul-body, spirit-flesh, heart-head, sacred-secular, Catholic-Protestant, Christian-Jew, divine-human. We need to realise that these are not states of perpetual opposition and that Jesus is not more present in one than the other.[5]

As suggested by Michael Morwood, we need to cultivate a genuine Christian spirituality which links our understanding of God, Jesus and ourselves in ways that are faithful to Jesus' teachings and the New Testament. One of our clearest pointers to this is given in John's first letter: 'God is love and when you live in love you live in God and God lives in you' (1 John 4:16). In other words, we need to believe that the sacred which we name as God is intimately part of each of us and love is the expression we give to it.[6]

Our pastoral leadership needs to recognise the gap that exists between current levels of popular faith and Church scholarship and realise that this is not well served by the often one-sided manner in which teaching is presented with minimal explanation. We need to be helped to know Jesus and Scripture better and made aware of how historical events, personalities, attitudes and thought patterns have shaped the way our faith has been packaged

---

[5] Morwood, Tomorrow's Catholic, p. 102.
[6] ibid., p. 103.

into a system of beliefs. This is an ongoing process for all of us. Truth is not a neatly parcelled commodity which has already been deposited with one section of the Church for them to disseminate amongst the rest.[7]

Many of us find it difficult to jump readily or unaided from the *Penny Catechism* level of detail to that contained in the 1994 *Catechism*, which, like many similar publications, seems to presume that every reader is an already enthusiastic adherent with some form of existing qualification in religious studies. In my view we require an 'intermediate solution' for an adult audience which uses an approach and language designed to generate interest, but acknowledges the need for a serious degree of catch-up for most people in the fields of theology and Church history.

We have the resources and the technology to produce and implement such a solution if there is the will to do so – a solution that captures the mood of the times in appealing to emotion as well as intellect and adopts a persuasive rather than a coercive manner of presentation. In terms of the Church itself and how we understand our respective roles and responsibilities, I consider that we might usefully reflect upon the following factors.

The nature of the Church

Vatican II describes the Church as first and foremost a work of God, a means of his presence in the world (*LG* #1). It is then stated to be a community of people who are called together to be 'one in the Spirit' (*LG* #9) and finally, and only then, it is referred to as a community with a structure and a hierarchy within it to help carry out its task. The ordering here is purposeful, not random.

The Church is therefore a spiritual community and a visible society, an earthly Church and a Church endowed with heavenly

---

[7] ibid., p. 121.

riches which combine to form a single complex reality that is both divine and human and centred on Jesus (*LG #8*). It is an entity that lives and grows in and through each of us as a result of our continuing relationship with the objective person of Jesus at a point in history and with the subjective experience of Jesus in the Christian community throughout our 'Spirit-led' history.

We need to maintain a balance between these objective and subjective dimensions, the visible and invisible dynamic of Jesus – the Jesus of history and the Jesus of faith. If we overemphasise the objective, there is the risk of excess centralism, legalism and conformity, whereas to overemphasise the subjective Jesus can lead to excess individualism in teaching without foundation or structure.

These were differing notions of Church which were examined by the nineteenth-century theologian Johann Mohler (1796–1830), who saw the former as being very much the Roman Catholic approach, where the scope for the individual was limited to obedience under authority. The latter reflected the position in many Protestant Churches, where teachings, cult and institution only came to life when they were an expression of the interior belief of the community.[8]

In Mohler's view, neither of these extremes was acceptable. His solution was to see the Church as a visible community of believers founded by Jesus in a body which now becomes his extension in time and space and where the divine and the human operate concurrently, in that it is not possible to have one without the other. Effectively, Mohler uses the doctrine of the 'hypostatic union' of the two natures of Jesus as an analogy to explain and understand the Church as Jesus made visible in us as the continuation of his incarnation.[9]

Later in the same century, our own Cardinal John Henry Newman (1801–90) offered the proposition that the triple office

---

[8] Philip J. Rosato, 'Between Christocentrism and Pneumatocentrism', *Heythrop Journal* 19, 1978, pp. 46–70.
[9] Peter Riga, 'The Ecclesiology of Johann Adam Mohler', *Theological Studies* 22, 1961, pp. 563–87.

usually attributed to the person of Jesus, namely, 'priest, prophet and king', was capable of being apportioned amongst different classes within the Church but taking care that one office should not dominate the others. He specifically cautioned against theology always having its own way on the grounds of being too hard, too intellectual, too exact to be always equitable or always compassionate.[10]

These several insights of Mohler and Newman found their way into the teaching of Vatican II and in my view they represent an ideal base upon which to devise a syllabus that enables us to better understand the nature and purpose of the Church and our part in it. It is an understanding that moves us from the notion of viewing ourselves simply as members of a religious institution to appreciating that through baptism we are that institution by virtue of being living components of the body of Christ.

The Eucharist

Vatican II teaches that the Eucharist is always an action of Jesus the priest and his body the Church (*SC #7*), that it was instituted by Jesus to be a memorial of his cross until he returns (*SC #47*) and a foretaste of the heavenly assembly in which we all hope to have a place (*SC #8*). Its effect is to draw us into Jesus' self-offering to his Father and into union with one another, so as sharers in his body and blood we accomplish our transformation into that which we receive (*LG #26*). I wonder how widely the import of these statements is appreciated within the Church in general?

The continual presence of Jesus in our earthly liturgy means that we are not a Church of any one place or time, but of all places and all times. To again cite the words of Henri deLubac,

---

[10] Referred to by Avery Dulles, *The Threefold Office in Newman's Ecclesiology* (Clarendon Press, 1990), p. 383.

it is the Eucharist that makes the Church and makes it what it is, namely, a sign and instrument of communion with God and of the unity of all people (*LG* #1). In the first millennium, this relationship between the Eucharist and the Church was seen as the ingredient which built and gave shape to the Christian community, but in subsequent years attention became directed more towards a study and analysis of the way in which Jesus is really present in the form of bread and wine. The link between the Eucharist and the Church became neglected.

The Eucharist is now categorised as one of the Church's seven sacraments, from which it might be assumed that it is the Church that makes the Eucharist and that it is just one example of the 'in-house benefits' which are made available for Church members. However, even by this definition there seems to be a contradiction in practice, as by insisting on an all-male celibate priesthood as the sole channel for its procurement, the Eucharist is being denied on a regular basis to many of the faithful around the world as a result of priest shortages.

I consider that the Eucharist, as the acknowledged source and summit of the Christian life (*LG* #11), demands a fuller explanation with a greater focus on its true ecclesial and community dimension.

Apostolicity

Under the guidance of the Holy Spirit, it was the apostles' eyewitness accounts of Jesus that gave the early Church its faith and centuries later their successor bishops formally determined the contents of the New Testament. Our claim to apostolic succession is highly important, but we need to be clear what the appointment of the original Twelve is likely to have meant to them and how this relates to us today.

Jesus selected a group of people with different personalities and backgrounds which combined to provide the collective talent he judged to be appropriate at that time for the leadership of the

Christian community. There is no evidence that he endowed them with perfect knowledge or any special insights for the purpose of their role. The whole of the Old Testament is a story about the uncertainties and struggles of a people as they journeyed towards the truth, so why would God suddenly decide to adopt a different plan and provide one small group with instant answers to every question, and for the emphasis thereafter to shift to being based on certainty and obedience?[11]

The commission which was given to the apostles was not in the form of a gift-wrapped product for them to share out amongst the rest. Each of us is called instead to live with the same questions, mystery, unknowns and seeming contradictions, but we have the assured and continuing support of the Spirit through whom we all, in our different ways, participate in the priesthood of Christ (*LG* #10).

We need to acknowledge that we do not yet hold the fullness of truth, nor are we able to make claims of absolute certainty for the poor human words we have used to set out our understanding of the inner life of God and to explain the exact manner in which Jesus is both divine and human. With God's grace, our level of discernment will continue to grow, but as suggested by Geoffrey Robinson, we need to find a balance between clear statements of beliefs which are essential to the identity of the Church and the need not to place more obligations on individuals than is necessary. To bow before the mystery of God rather than always attempting to define it is an acceptable option.[12]

Collegiality

The appointment of the Twelve signified a new community which existed in the communal union of the group, whereby each

---

[11] See Robinson, *Confronting Power and Sex in the Catholic Church*, p. 123.
[12] ibid., p. 238.

individual member had significance not in his own right but because of being in union with the others. This collegiate character and structure continues today in that the office of bishop is not conferred in isolation, but is held by each bishop in virtue of belonging to the Collegium as the post-apostolic continuation of the apostles.

The bishops in the early Church were responsible for their 'local churches', but were also conscious of their collective responsibility for the Church as a whole, and this quickly led to the practice of bishops' synods or councils to consider and resolve important issues. To be effective each bishop had to really and faithfully represent his local church, 'so that through him part of the Church's plenitude is inserted into the totality of the Church's unity'.[13]

The concept of episcopal collegiality was made visible and reaffirmed by Vatican II. It was shown here to be grounded in the Eucharist, in that wherever bishops in communion with each other and the successor to St Peter may be in the world, they all preside at the same unique sacrifice at their particular altars, surrounded by their priests and people (*SC* #41). Bishops installed throughout the world live in communion with one another and the Roman Pontiff in a bond of unity, charity and peace (*LG* #22).

Unfortunately, this is not the manner in which collegiality is currently allowed to operate in the face of what I can only describe as a 'Rome-centred oligarchy'. Under this arrangement, all decisions are reached in the centre and edicts are then transmitted for unquestioning implementation by individual bishops or groups of bishops. Not only is this at variance with the explicit wishes of the Council, it also runs contrary to the theology of the episcopal office itself and can often undermine the pastoral effectiveness of each bishop in his local church.

---

[13] Joseph Ratzinger, *The Pastoral Implications of Episcopal Collegiality* (Concilium, 1965), p. 27.

The Papacy

The role which Jesus conferred on St Peter can be seen to be specific, but still within the same framework as the appointment of the other eleven witnesses. The title of 'rock' was applied to St Peter, which I interpret as being for him to act as a sound foundation, a point of reference, a symbol of unity for his fellow appointees. This seems to be supported by Jesus' exhortation, 'Simon, Simon! Satan you must know, has got his wish to sift you all like wheat: but I have prayed for you, Simon, that your faith may not fail, and once you have recovered, you in your turn must strengthen your brothers' (Luke 22:31–32).

In other words, the primacy of Peter and in succession each Bishop of Rome is not opposed to the collegial character of the Church, but can be understood as a primacy of communion in the midst of the Church living as a community and understanding itself as such. It means the faculty and the right to decide authoritatively, within the network of communication, where the Word of the Lord is witnessed correctly and consequently where there is true communion. It presupposes the *communion ecclesiarum* and can be understood correctly only in reference to it.[14]

In practice today, there is a presumption, if not an insistence, that on all matters of importance Catholics must first look to the Pope for guidance and direction. It is the Pope who determines what is and what is not a matter of importance and with the present structure of the Church it is the Pope alone who has the power to make changes.[15] The Papacy and everything that is associated with the office of Bishop of Rome appears to have become credited with a quasi-oracular status and it is interesting to observe how frequently these days the title of 'Pope' is superseded by the appellation 'Holy Father'. One wonders where this might lead.

---

[14] ibid., p. 25.
[15] Robinson, *Confronting Power and Sex in the Catholic Church*, p. 8.

St Peter was chosen by Jesus to lead the original Twelve, but not to be patterned on the model of an absolute monarchy or to assume sole and total responsibility for everything pertaining to the Church – in the words of Eamon Duffy, for each Pope to act as the equivalent of a CEO in a multinational corporation, ensuring brand uniformity in all local branches, hiring and firing middle management and dictating the nature and availability of the company product.[16]

In my opinion, there is an imbalance here which is unhealthy, and under the supposed signature of the Pope we are called to accept ever-increasing directives from Rome covering all aspects of Church life with the expectation of complete uniformity in implementation. This too is at variance with the Council's wish for 'inculturation', the ongoing interaction between faith and local culture to the advantage of both. I believe that the whole issue of the Papacy and its acquired administrative 'accoutrements' calls for prayerful examination and resolution in the context of the Church's long and ongoing apostolic tradition.

Outreach

Over several centuries, the focus of our pastoral leadership has been to isolate and protect the Catholic faith together with the Catholic faithful from all social, intellectual and political innovation and change. However well intentioned this may have been at the time, Vatican II signalled a different approach and its 'Constitution on the Church in the Modern World' (*Gaudium et Spes*) forcefully set out the case for us to re-engage with the world, not as competitors but as fellow contributors in the journey of human progress.

We are now called to present our faith story honestly and confidently and to give witness to this in the way we behave in

---

[16] Duffy, *Faith of our Fathers*, p. 61.

response to our beliefs. I believe we need to begin with more open and informative teaching from our pastoral leadership, orientated exclusively on Jesus as our beginning and our future. In the final analysis, we have to accept that we are unable to convey the whole notion of God as a result of our limited human intellect, but we can still offer meaningful insights for people's further consideration. What is well within our competence is to be able to offer our time, our help, our support and our compassion to those in need. After all, is that not what Jesus did?

To leave the final words to Pope Benedict XVI:

> True renewal of the Church will always consist only of the removal of redundant historical accretions (new ones will ever again grow up unnoticed) so that the pure image of its original reality may shine forth. Mere concessions to the times or mere 'modernization' are always false attempts at renewal which at first arouse enthusiasm but are soon seen to be delusive, for in the competition for modernization the Church will never come up first. In the course of history, the well-intentioned modernizations have always proved very soon to be obstacles which tied the Church to a definite epoch and had a paralysing effect on the power of its message.
>
> Although the renewal of the Church can come only from turning to its origin, it must be something altogether different from restoration, the romantic glorification of the past, which would be just as un-Christian as mere modernisation. This is so because the historical Jesus on whom the Church is based is at the same time the Coming Christ in whom the Church hopes; because Christ is not only the Christ of yesterday but also the Christ of today and for ever (see Hebrews 13:8).[17]

Viva Il Papa!

---

[17] Ratzinger, *The Pastoral Implications of Episcopal Collegiality* (Concilium, 1965), p. 31.

Closure

At the beginning of this book I admitted to being a cradle Catholic who was still committed to the faith that my parents had handed on to me as a child. I wish to end with an even stronger expression of my gratitude to them and my determination to remain an active Catholic.

In the intervening pages, I have attempted to fulfil my obligation under Canon Law 'to manifest to the sacred Pastors my views on matters which concern the good of the Church' (#212). Over and above this I have sought to portray something of my continued enthusiasm for being a Catholic where the high point for me is always a feeling of 'oneness' when participating at Mass in different places around the world, irrespective of the variations in setting, language, music and culture.

There are, of course, other occasions when being Catholic gives rise to frustrations in the way teachings are sometimes presented or opportunities are missed to better clarify and promote the essential message of Jesus both within the Church and in society at large. Many of my criticisms are directed towards our pastoral leadership, but given their responsibility as teachers and the all-pervasive position which they have also assumed within the Church, this seems unavoidable. Such criticisms are, however, intended to be constructive and are made with a sincere hope that they strike some responsive chord and that under the guidance of the Holy Spirit we can all continue on our journey as the body of Christ beyond the purely written word of Vatican II.

Our goal must be to remain attuned to the joys and hopes, the grief and anguish of the peoples of our time. If we can achieve this in some small way, our visible contribution to the world will be the love of God expressed by the way in which we continue to live out the incarnation of Jesus.

Appendix

The documents of the Second Vatican Council

The Council produced 16 documents made up of four Constitutions, nine Decrees and three Declarations. The difference between a Constitution and a Decree springs from the different levels or strata found in Christian teaching. Some beliefs such as the Trinity are fundamental and essential to the faith and such matters are dealt with in a Constitution. Other matters like the relationship between bishops and priests, while binding, are not essential for salvation and are dealt with in Decrees.

Both Constitutions and Decrees may contain what is thought of as 'development of doctrine', i.e. where the Church's teaching evolves under the guidance of the Holy Spirit in the light of new insights and advances of knowledge. Declarations deal with matters that merely cast light on existing laws and governances of the Church.

The Constitutions

'Constitution on the Sacred Liturgy', *Sacrosanctum Concilium* (December 1963)
'Dogmatic Constitution on Divine Revelation', *Dei Verbum* (November 1964)
'Dogmatic Constitution on the Church', *Lumen Gentium* (November 1964)

'Pastoral Constitution on the Church in the Modern World', *Gaudium et Spes* (December 1965)

The Decrees

'Decree on the Mass Media', *Inter Mirifica* (December 1963)
'Decree on Ecumenism', *Unitatis Redintegrato* (November 1964)
'Decree on Catholic Eastern Churches', *Orientalium Ecclesiarum* (November 1964)
'Decree on the Ministry and Life of Priests', *Prebyterorum Ordinis* (November 1964)
'Decree on the Pastoral Office of Bishops in the Church', *Christus Dominus* (October 1965)
'Decree on the training of Priests', *Optatam Totius* (October 1965)
'Decree on the up to date Renewal of Religious Life' *Perfectae Caritatis* (October 1965)
'Decree on the Apostolate of the Lay People', *Apostolicum Actuositatem* (November 1965)
'Decree on the Church's Missionary Activity', *Ad Gentes Divinitus* (December 1965)

The Declarations

'Declaration on the Relation of the Church to Non-Christian Religions', *Nostra Aetate* (October 1965)
'Declaration on Christian Education', *Gravissimum Educationis* (October 1965)
'Declaration on Religious Freedom', *Dignitatis Humanae* (December 1965)

Bibliography

Audet, Jean-Paul, *Structures of Christian Priesthood* (Sheed & Ward Stagbooks, 1967).

Brown, Dan, *The Da Vinci Code* (Bantam Press, 2003).

Burns, Robert A., *Roman Catholicism after Vatican II* (Georgetown University Press, 2001).

Butler, Christopher, *In the Light of the Council* (Darton, Longman and Todd, 1969).

Castle, Tony, *Good Pope John and His Council* (Kevin Mayhew, 2006).

Clark, Stephen B., *Building Christian Communities* (Ave Maria Press, 1972).

Congar, Yves, ed. A. Stacpoole, *A Last Look at the Council: Vatican II by Those Who Were There* (Geoffrey Chapman, 1986).

Coriden, James A., *The Parish in Catholic Tradition* (Paulist Press, 1997).

Coriden, James A., *Canon Law as Ministry* (Paulist Press, 2000).

Coulson, John, *Newman on the Church – His Final View, Its Origins and Influence, An Oxford Symposium* (SPCK, 1967).

Daley, Gabriel, 'Faith and Theology', *The Tablet*, April/May 1981.

DeLubac, Henri, *Catholicism: Christ the Common Destiny of Man* (Ignatius Press, 1988).

Duffy, Eamon, *Faith of our Fathers* (Continuum, 2004).

Dulles, Avery, 'Authority and Conscience', in *Readings in Moral Theology*, No. 6 (Paulist Press, 1988).

Dulles, Avery, *The Threefold Office in Newman's Ecclesiology* (Clarendon Press, 1990).

Durrwell, Francis-Xavier, *The Spirit of the Father and the Son* (St Paul Publications, 1990).

Dyche, W., *Transcendental Christology* in, Outstanding Christian Thinkers – Karl Rahner (Geoffrey Chapman, 1992).

Gunton, Colin E., *Father, Son and Holy Spirit* (T. & T. Clark, 2003).

Hill, Edmund, *Ministry and Authority in the Catholic Church* (Geoffrey Chapman, 1988).

Jaki, Stanley L. (ed.), *Conscience and Papacy* (Real View Books, 2002).

Kilby, Karen, *Karl Rahner* (Fount, 1997).

Komonchak, Joseph, *Theology and Culture at Mid-Century: The Example of Henri deLubac* (Theological Studies 51, 1990).

LaCugna, Catherine Mowry, *The Trinitarian Mystery of God* (Fortress, 1991).

Lightbound, Christopher, *The Church Then and Now* (St Paul's, 2004).

Loret, Pierre, *The Story of the Mass* (Liguori Publications, 1982).

Lucas, Ernest, *Can We Believe Genesis Today?* (Inter-Varsity Press, 2001).

McGrath, Alister, and Joanna Collicut McGrath, *The Dawkins Delusion* (SPCK, 2007).

McPartlan, Paul, *Eucharist: The Body of Christ* (Catholic Truth Society, 2004).

McPartlan, Paul, *Sacrament of Salvation* (T. & T. Clark, 1995).

Morwood, Michael, *Tomorrow's Catholic* (Spectrum Publications, 1997).

Muggeridge, Malcolm, *Jesus, the Man Who Lives* (William Collins, 1975).

Musto, Ronald G., *The Catholic Peace Tradition* (Orbis Books, 1986).

O'Collins, Gerald, *Jesus our Redeemer* (Oxford University Press, 2007).

O'Collins, Gerald, *Jesus, A Portrait* (Darton, Longman and Todd, 2008).

Provost, James, 'Promoting and Protecting the Right of Christians', *The Jurist*, 1986.

Ratzinger, Joseph, *The Pastoral Implications of Episcopal Collegiality* (Concilium, 1965).

Richards, Michael, *A People of Priests* (Darton, Longman and Todd, 1995).

Riga, Peter, 'The Ecclesiology of Johann Adam Mohler', *Theological Studies* 22, 1961.

Robinson, Geoffrey, *Confronting Power and Sex in the Catholic Church* (The Columbia Press, 2007).

Rosato, Philip J., 'Between Christocentrism and Pneumatocentrism' *Heythrop Journal* 19, 1978.

Rush, Ormond, *Still Interpreting Vatican II* (Paulist Press, 2004).

Tanner, Norman P., *The Councils of the Church: A Short History* (Crossroad Publishing, 2001).

Winter, M., On Yves Congar, *Clergy Review*, 55 (1970).

Wright, N.T., *Evil and the Justice of God* (SPCK, 2006).

Other references

Catechism of the Catholic Church (Geoffrey Chapman, 1994).

Collins Dictionary and Thesaurus (Collins, 1987).

Come O Holy Spirit (Catholic Truth Society, 1950), by a Sister of Notre Dame.

Albert Einstein, Religion and Science, www.sacred-texts.com/aor/einstein/einsci.htm)

Modern Catholic Encyclopedia, eds. Michael Glazier and Monika Hellwig (Gill and Macmillan, 1994).

New Bible (Catholic Truth Society, 2007).

Penny Catechism (Catholic Truth Society, latest ed. 1997).

Vatican Council II, ed. A. Flannery (Costello Publishing, 1996).

Westminster Year Book 2009 (Westminster Roman Catholic Diocese Trustee © WRCDT 2010), 59th edition.

Your Faith (Redemptorist Publications, 1990).